HEALING THE HINDU MUSLIM DIVIDE

MOIN QAZI

INDIA • SINGAPORE • MALAYSIA

ISBN 979-8-89277-876-3

Contents

The Trauma of Partition

The Hindu-Muslim divide is the toughest challenge facing the Indian subcontinent, and it will continue to do so in times to come. It has suddenly flared up and doesn't give hope of getting doused easily. One of the reasons is that despite being a minority in a new homeland, Muslims have become a strong, assertive minority. At the same time, Hindus have become extremely aggressive and assertive and are keen to see that their faith becomes the national faith. The two nations have coexisted uneasily since the 1947 Partition of India, which ended almost two centuries of British rule in the region and led to the largest mass migration in human history. The Partition created the independent nations of Muslim-majority Pakistan and Hindu-majority India.

It is now hard to look back without horror at the savagery of the country's division. The genocides and mass displacement worsened as people sought frantically to be on the "right" side of the lines the British were to draw across their homeland. In a frantic headlong rush of mass movements for freedom and the Partition, the British emerged as absolutely inept in handling the crisis that followed. Before World War II, they had no intention of acquiring power so rapidly or at all.

The creation and perpetuation of Hindu-Muslim animosity was the most significant outcome of the British policy of divide and rule. They were experts in drawing maps of other countries which reflected newly drawn territories; they had done it in the Middle East after World War I, and they did it again in India. The Partition was the major result of the collapse of British authority in India in 1947. The idea of the Partition was on the table in the first place because the British had already applied it in the process of decolonising Ireland and were discussing using it in Palestine. They considered it a useful compromise for ensuring all territory wound up within the British Commonwealth after devolution.

In the 75 years since the Partition, territorial disputes between India and Pakistan have continued to simmer, erupting into four wars and ongoing cross-border attacks. The Partition is still raw for many of those who experienced it firsthand. As each year passes, friction continues to grow.

The Partition may have occurred over 75 years ago, but the impact and legacy of British colonialism and the division of the subcontinent remain a significant force in the present-day geopolitics of the region. What's more, it has shaped the lives of the survivors, their children, and their grandchildren, who are dispersed all over the world. It demonstrates how major historical events such as the Partition stay with us and ultimately shape the lives of those who descend from it. Across the Indian subcontinent, communities that had coexisted for almost a millennium attacked each other in a terrifying outbreak of sectarian violence. The polarisation of Hindus and Muslims occurred during just a couple of decades of the twentieth century, but by the middle of the century, it was so complete that many on both sides believed that adherents of the two religions couldn't live together peacefully.

For half a century or more before emancipation, nationalists of both the great religious communities had stridently asserted that communal antipathy was illusory—a mere creation of the British Raj, allegedly following the old Roman maxim of "divide and rule." History since independence has shown with tragic clarity that antagonism between Muslims and Hindus is much more deeply rooted than what most strategists thought.

In recent years, religiously inspired nationalist movements have gained prominence in several countries. Few cases are more emblematic of this phenomenon than India on account of its unique features, such as its size and its democratic credentials over a long history. India is home to one-quarter of the world's voters and one-sixth of humanity, making it the largest democracy. There was huge collateral damage as a result of the actual Partition. People who lived together like families found their relations torn asunder. Friendships were destroyed, and minds and hearts were torn apart. Mobs attacked refugees and villagers, set buildings on fire, looted homes and businesses, and committed mass murder, rape, and butchery.

In colonial India, religious identities first began to emerge within political groups, and the challenges faced by Hindus and Muslims began to heighten. Religious conflict was the biggest challenge India faced at the time, and this was emphasised through the constant rivalry that developed between the two primary, authoritative political actors at the time: the Indian Congress Party (INC) and the All-India Muslim League (Muslim League). These parties were each confronted with the other's opposing ideology, which ultimately resulted in British India being divided into two independent states—India and Pakistan.

The British Crown rule in India was established in the mid-nineteenth century. The academic community has extensively explored the impacts of colonialism on Hindu-Muslim relationships both pre-independence and post-independence. The traditional interpretation believes that the colonial past was instrumental in recognising Muslim identities, which resulted in the Partition of British India in 1947.

In the chaos of those first days, when ancient principalities were pledging to join one of the two nations, Kashmir's final status was by no means certain. The Muslim majority rose repeatedly against the Hindu Maharaja and his plans to remain independent. Pakistani tribesmen raided to wrest control, and India marched troops into the region with a promise to keep the peace and hold a referendum. Tens of thousands of Muslims were slaughtered by Hindu mobs in the southern Jammu region, while hundreds of thousands more were driven from their homes to Pakistan or Pakistani-controlled Kashmir.

It has lately become fashionable to blame the current conflict between Hindus and Muslims on the British and the British Raj's colonial policies. The colonial project of 'divide et impera' (divide and rule) fomented religious antagonisms for political reasons that didn't facilitate continued imperial rule until it culminated in 1947. Some argue that the very religious identities of Hindus and Muslims in the subcontinent were a result of British strategy. British, and as such, the subsequent strife between these groups was an extension of this policy.

It is widely debated that most of South Asia's contemporary geopolitical and ethno-religious problems, including the Kashmir conflict, the division of British India into India and Pakistan, and communal strife between Hindus and Muslims, are the result of Western influence. In this view, everyone in South Asia lived in relative harmony together before the 19th century. Often, British policies such as the 1909 decision to give Indian Muslims a separate electorate from Hindus in local elections, as well as the British role in India's 1947 Partition, are cited as part of the strategy to sow conflict between Indians.

Together, the two communities can bridge the gap between cultures and forge a way to become more open and tolerant. We can innovate and foster a new meaning of peace and inclusiveness through education, art, and conversational exchange. We must realize that to create long-term change, we must spread ideas that have the power to evolve societies.

India was established in 1947 as a pluralist nation, home to people of many sects, religions, and ethnicities. The country's constitution did not provide any special claim over the state or its territory to any one of them—including the Hindus, who make up roughly 80 per cent of the population.

Most examples in history of such fanatical approaches are few and far between. History can be better understood if we avoid focusing on those exceptions that have tainted civilizations as role models. This can help in getting a more rational picture of rulers and their kingdoms. A careful analysis of history will reveal that several Muslim rulers rehabilitated Hindu populations and promoted their culture and civilization. This syncretism can be seen throughout history. The reciprocal support between Hindu and Muslim rulers has helped in the promotion of a unique brand of Indian civilization. Had the British not been steeped in intentions, Indian culture and learning would have reached great peaks. It is now for our sages to design how to rebuild the ancient glory which still glows in our long history.

British Strategy

Before and during the war, the British ensured that by the time departure came, the Muslim League was strong enough to sustain its demand for a separate homeland for Muslims, and the prospects of a united India surviving a British exit had essentially faded. The divide-and-rule policy proved to be a marvellous device to reinforce British rule in India.

Meanwhile, having secured their aim of having both newly independent countries in the Commonwealth, British officials tried to hurry up events at every turn. The hasty dismantling of the imperial state not only made it harder to address the violence but also made much of the violence possible in the first place. The imperial state turned out to be a failure, offering little support to administrators trying to deal with routine local politics. The British Army began to depart just when India's army was being divided and could not be relied on to manage violence.

On 14 August 1947, as 200 years of British rule came to an end, India was divided into two independent states, Muslim-majority Pakistan and Hindu-majority India. But within hours, the long-awaited transition of power—and the Partition of India into two nations—became a nightmare as simmering tensions, stoked by divisive colonial rule, boiled over. The birth of the new nations witnessed an abortion since freedom came with the horrors of the Partition in which millions of people lost their lives. Today, everywhere one looks in India, one sees political deterioration and religious turmoil.

It was one of the most painful births in modern history. On August 14 and 15, 1947, Pakistan and India became dominions of the British Crown—with the understanding they would ultimately become fully independent. But Mountbatten refused to issue the maps until two days later in an attempt to keep the international focus on Britain's benevolence.

An Inept Partition

The task of dividing the two nations was assigned to Sir Cyril Radcliffe, a lawyer who had never visited India before and knew nothing of its culture. He could barely grasp the challenge that lay ahead of him, and he made the biggest mess in modern political history. Radcliffe drew up his maps in less than five weeks, dividing provinces, districts, villages, homes, and hearts—and promptly scuttled his return to India, never realising the massacre that his work would result in due to his sheer callousness. The British

Empire simply crumbled in disorder. The British were bothered by the catastrophe of a lost nation and, worse, the humanitarian crisis. It would be lost in their headlong rush to the exits.

More than 12 million people were displaced as Muslims in Punjab and Bengal fled across the hastily drawn borders by Radcliffe, the man ill-equipped to handle such a humongous geographical division of territories and populations into two separate nations. In the sectarian violence that ensued, 2 million people were killed, tens of thousands of women were raped and abducted, homes were plundered, and villages were torched. Two decades after the new Muslim nation of Pakistan was sundered, Auden wrote of how Cyril Radcliffe—the British barrister who had "never set eyes on this land he was called to partition"—had been assigned the task of separating "two peoples fanatically at odds, with their different diets and incompatible gods."It's a jaunty line, a little dated in its Orientalism, but it encapsulates the deep-rooted differences—between Muslims, on the one hand, and Hindus and Sikhs, on the other—that were to find bloodthirsty expression in the course of Partition.

There were roughly 35 million Muslims who opted to live on the Indian side of the Radcliffe Line in the aftermath of Partition; it was a gamble for most Muslims. They didn't want to go to a theocratic state. Indeed, when Pakistan finally adopted a constitution, nine years after the Partition, it proclaimed Islam as the state religion. The promise of a pluralist India, as envisaged by the country's founders, trumped the warnings of Muslims that a Muslim minority would inevitably be subordinate to the majority of Hindus. Muslim leaders did not use reason and were carried away by emotional sentiments.

The suddenness, scale, and ferocity of the violence that erupted in 1947 were still shocking. As historians and writers such as

NisidHajary and Saadat Hassan Manto have noted, it was a time when the normal mores of civilization were suspended, and neighbors massacred each other without a thought. Most Muslims were not prepared for the holocaust and were horrified. Almost everybody recalled the words of Maulana Azad, who had prophesied that once partition took place, India would be ruled by an unadulterated Hindu Raj, and Muslims would overnight become second-class citizens. It was the euphoria of most North Indian Muslims that independence would give them freedom and autonomy. They never realized the other side of the picture.

Today, India's Muslims are apprehensive. Earlier sectarian violence *was usually a phenomenon* orchestrated to win elections and was always followed by a process of reconciliation. But the picture changed suddenly, and violence was the call of the day, with peace disrupted. Mayhem ruled the streets, and even women and children were not spared. For India's Muslims, their consolation is that their status is better than that of Hindus and the Muslim League's fears and fantasies, which seem to be slowly spinning their way into the orbit of Indian reality.

As the great WH Auden wrote of Radcliffe:

Unbiased at least he was when he arrived on his mission,
Having never set eyes on the land he was called to Partition
Between two people fanatically at odds,
With their different diets and incompatible gods.

The Great Massacre

India never fully recovered from the partition, which resulted from differences along religious lines, and communal prejudices continue to run deep. Politicians of all stripes made sincere attempts to dampen antagonisms through public campaigns emphasizing communal harmony. However, the ruling Bharatiya Janata Party—

and their right-wing Hindu grassroots organizations—were steeped in nationalism and saw the Muslim minority as a threat to the Hindu majority, responding with violent remedies. Conflicts between Hindus and Muslims go back centuries and were aggravated by British colonial policy of "divide and rule," leading to the 1947 partition. The two religions were, to begin with, about as different as two belief systems, and it was clear that the fault lines between the two communities were drawn, and they could not maintain any cordiality between each other. They suddenly became enemies after such close relations just a few days or weeks back. Islam is monotheistic, proselytising, anti-idolatrous, fiercely doctrinal, with strong ideas about heresy. Hinduism is pantheistic, uninterested in converting unbelievers, an immense aggregation of different gods, rites, superstitions, and beliefs.

There was never going to be a neat fit between the two. For nearly a millennium, Islam has always symbolized itself as the religion and the badge of the subcontinent's invaders, whereas Hindus were a cultural race that marked itself as a unique civilization. There is no doubt that often aspects of Hindu and Islamic, particularly Persian and Turkic, cultures influenced each other. At the village level, Hindus and Muslims shared a plethora of customs and beliefs, at times even jointly worshipping the same saint. Ajmer and its holy sites are a case in point.

On its surface, the August 1947 creation of two self-governing nations was a victory for those who longed for self-determination. But simmering secular tensions and a severely mismanaged transition turned Britain's historic exit from the colony into a bloodbath. Communal rioting had broken out, with mobs of Hindus and Muslims fighting each other and terrorising people. Muslims did not feel safe anymore. Everyone's luggage was on the roads. Five generations of culture and tradition were being sold on the streets.

The Worst Human Catastrophe

The chaos, confusion, and religious violence that accompanied the cleaving of Pakistan from India resulted in the deaths of up to two million people and unleashed one of history's largest displacements, with Hindus and Muslims from once-mixed communities rushing in opposite directions to new homelands created along religious lines. What should have been a joyful occasion was marred by the ghastly slaughter of half a million people and the uprooting of about 15 million men, women, and children. Overnight, Hindu and Muslim neighbours became fearful of one another. Mob violence broke out, leaving hundreds of thousands dead. Muslims and Hindus lived in mixed communities throughout the area. Although the agreement required no relocation, about 15 million people moved or were forced to move, and between half a million to 2 million died in the ensuing violence. More than a million people died in the savagery that accompanied the freedom of India and Pakistan; some 17 million were displaced, and countless properties were destroyed and looted. There was a wave and avalanche of paranoia that seemed to generate massive violence, strife, and distress. There was uncontrollable fear in everyday life. Whatever religious justifications may have been at play in the violence, many actions emerged from a sense of desperate need for survival in a harrowing environment.

However painful the political environment has become, it should not surprise any observer. Long before the British conquered India, the Hindus were not happy with their Muslim Moghuls and those who embraced the faith of these rulers. For their part, Muslims were a martial race and scorned those with a lesser muscular build even though they were intellectually more endowed than others. Moreover, even after the Partition, there was a lack of greater statecraft that could subjugate the widespread breakdown of law and order. There still is no political balm to heal the hereditary strains between the two great communal factions.

The Hindu-Muslim Divide

The friction between Hindus and Muslims has become a permanent feature of Indian life, and periodic bouts of bloody rioting may continue to remain common. However, since the rise of Prime Minister Narendra Modi and the BJP, violence against Muslims has increased. There are several distortions in the historical accounts of both Hindus and Muslims, and these are creating friction among communities that have lived in harmony for centuries. It requires a saner understanding of the deeper fault lines, or else the priorities of our country will be jeopardised. For centuries and decades, Muslim and Hindu communities have lived side by side as friends, colleagues, and business partners - but unease among them has been growing in recent times.

The creation of Pakistan was a product of a surprise idea heard publicly just a few months before. It was invented by a few Muslim intellectuals in 1933 who claimed that there were two distinct nations in India; this idea was then adopted by the Muslim League at its historic meeting in Lahore in 1940 as implying an independent sovereign "homeland" for Indian Muslims. The Partition also marked bitterness between the populations that once closely loved and lived with each other.

There were attempts by Muslims to mobilize and integrate Hindus into their kingdoms to give a secular edge to their rule. However, this could never establish deeper roots into the local soil. No matter how much syncretism and fluidity there was, it was impossible for India's two sets of elites—the Hindu Brahmin-Kshatriya combined on one hand, and the Perso-Turkic Muslims—to agree upon which aspects of India's history to draw upon to build modern identities.

Akbar and several Mughal rulers patronized Brahmins and sages, while Muslims served in elite roles in the armies of southern Hindus. But the cultural orientations of Hindu and Muslim states were different, and invariably, Hindu and Muslim rulers in modern India would stick to their syncretic backgrounds.

The Sepoy Mutiny

In 1857, Indian soldiers mutinied—prompting the British government to come out with an aggressive response to subjugate the mutiny's attack. The newly established British Raj appointed officials—many of whom had never set foot in India before—to keep its colony in line. Those privileged British administrators and their families lived in wealth and luxury, while most Indians lived in poverty. The British had been horrified, during the Revolt of 1857, to see Hindus and Muslims fighting side by side and under each other's command against the foreign oppressor. This was the first demonstration of strong Hindu-Muslim unity, which the British finally broke for their vested interests. They vowed this would not happen again. A systematic policy of fomenting separate consciousness among the two communities was initiated, with shrewd overtness of the British. Its primary objective was to sow distress between the two common nations so that the British could use one against the other with prudent political craftsmanship. When the restricted franchise was granted to Indians, the British created separate communal electorates so that Muslim voters could vote for Muslim candidates for Muslim seats. The seeds of division were sown to prevent a unified nationalist movement that could overthrow the British.

The British were horrified during the Revolt of 1857 to see Hindus and Muslims fighting side by side and under each other's command. They vowed that this would not happen again. "Divide et imperia" was an old Roman maxim, and it would become ours," wrote Lord Elphinstone. A systematic strategy was designed to foment communalism and create a separate consciousness among the two communities, with overt British sponsorship. Separate communal electorates were established to perpetuate and reinforce Hindu-Muslim antagonism. This extraordinary unity frantically unnerved the firangees and made them realise that if their rule was to continue in India, it could happen only when Hindus and Muslims, the two largest religious communities, were divided along communal lines. The systematic divide and rule that the British learned from this war made them formulate a policy to divide the secular populations into several divisions and incite conflicts among them that finally resulted in the Partition of India.

India's Secularism Under Siege

> *Hindu-Muslim unity means not unity only between Hindus and Mussulmans, but between all those who believe India to be their home, no matter to what faith they belong... It is a daily-growing plant, as yet in delicate infancy, requiring special care and attention.*
>
> **– Mahatma Gandhi in Young India, May 11, 1925**

The Indian prime minister was speaking from the historic MughalRed Fort in New Delhi, and the event marked the 400th birth anniversary celebrations of Guru Tegh Bahadur, the ninth Sikh guru. The occasion and the venue, in many ways, were appropriate. Modi reminded people of India's most despised Muslim ruler, who died over 300 years ago. "Back then, Aurangzeb severed many heads, but he could not shake our faith," Modi said during his address. His invocation of the 17th-century Mughal emperor was not a mere blip.

Aurangzeb remains buried deep in the annals of India's complex history. But the country's modern rulers are now resurrecting him as a brutal oppressor of Hindus, using it as a rallying cry for Hindu nationalists and Hindu-Muslim animosity. They believe that they must salvage India from the so-called shame of Muslims. We must not forget the authoritatively documented fact that the first war of Indian independence was fought under the banner of the Mughal Emperor Bahadur Shah Zafar, and people of all religious denominations rallied together and challenged the greatest imperialist power, Britain, during India's first war of independence, which began on May 10, 1857. Moreover, Rani Laxmibai of Jhansi and Nana Saheb also fought under the Mughal banner and not under the Peshwas. The 1857 Hindu-Muslim unity was the first shock that shook the British Empire.

India is home to some 200 million Muslims, who make up the predominantly Hindu country's largest minority group. They are scattered across almost every part of India and are part of a systemic anti-Muslim fury that has descended since Prime Minister Narendra Modi first assumed power in 2014. Though India's communal fractures date back to its bloody Partition in 1947, most Indians trace the roots of the latest religious fault lines to the temple city of Ayodhya in northern India, where the Hindu nationalist movement was galvanised in 1992 after Hindu mobs demolished a historic mosque to make way for a temple.

For devout Hindus, the new temple is a rejoinder for their humiliation at the hands of the Mughal Empire. Ayodhya is said to be the birthplace of Ram and the setting for the Sanskrit epic Ramayana. The BJP has argued that it was essential to build a temple on the site to heal the "civilisational wounds unleashed by Muslim rulers. While Mr Modi's status will be raised among his Hindu nationalist supporters for delivering the temple, Not all rulers were savage or barbaric, but the rumour machine run by the Hindu chauvinists painted a very Muslim ruler in dark colours.

Seventy-five years later, those warnings have gained a new prescience. , India remains a secular state and plural democracy. Religious minorities account for roughly 20 per cent of the country's 1.4 billion people, who include about 200 million Muslims and 28 million Christians. But the inclusivity is very thin; deeper and deeper below runs an undercurrent of Hindu nationalism that has been reinforced during the rule of Prime Minister Narendra Modi. The concern shared by religious minorities, as well as by more secular-minded liberals within the Hindu majority, is that the country's secular and inclusive ethos is already beyond repair.

Democracy has always been a strong asset for India, but Narendra Modi's hyper-nationalism is reconfiguring the political tool of India. When Narendra Modi entered the Indian polity after his electoral victory that catapulted him to the premiership as the democratic topmost leader, he bowed down at the steps that led him to what he mentioned as the "temple of democracy". This reverential gesture not only acknowledged the will of the people but was also a ritualised celebration of India's established democratic institutions. But as time proved later, this was not a sincere ideal. India, as the "mother of democracy," became a political motif that helped Modi capitalise on India's democratic credentials even as it bolstered nationalist pride.

History has demonstrated with tragic clarity that animosity between Muslims and Hindus is much more deeply rooted than one can imagine. The ink was not yet dry on the 1947 act of sovereignty before what had been one great single nation under British rule became split into two sullenly hostile countries, Pakistan and India.

Though independence began to appear within India's grasp, divisions between the Indian National Congress and the Muslim League deepened. Gandhi and Jawaharlal Nehru had long believed an independent India should be a single, unified nation. But although the Muslim League also supported home rule, its leader Muhammad Ali Jinnah publicly abandoned the cause of a unified India in 1940 and decided to claim a separate Muslim state.

The Follies of Mountbatten

The last British Viceroy, Earl Mountbatten, who held the deciding power, affecting more than five hundred separate states and 93 million people, declared, with the prior approval of the governments of both India and Pakistan, the considerations that should decide the states' choice. The overriding factor was to be the will of the people concerned. In cases where the ruler's wishes conflicted or were likely to conflict on communal, religious, or other grounds with those of his subjects, the latter's will, to be given a free, prompt opportunity to express itself, should prevail. Mountbatten convinced leaders to agree to the creation of two new states, Hindu-majority India and Muslim-majority Pakistan. But although he was given a year to complete his task, he rushed the schedule—giving Cyril Radcliffe, a British lawyer who had never set foot in India, just five weeks to divide the country in two and demarcate the new nations' borders.

Princely states could decide which nation they wanted to join, and Radcliffe and his team were otherwise told to draw boundaries that respected religious majorities and prioritised contiguous borders. The "Radcliffe Line" was easy to draw in areas with a distinct majority, but Radcliffe soon found that the religious groups were dispersed throughout the country, and it may not be possible to arrive at a feasible solution. In areas like Bengal and Punjab, which had near-equal Hindu and Muslim populations, drawing a line proved particularly difficult.

The absurdity and heartbreak of the overnight creation of new borders are reflected in the literature of the two nations. In a short story by Saadat Hasan Manto, a writer who lived in India and was forced to leave for Pakistan, the two nations decide to exchange patients from their mental institutions, just as they had exchanged prisoners of war. A patient keeps trying to find out where his village, Toba Tek Singh, now lies.

India's religious fault lines have become more pronounced under Modi. Scores of Muslims have been lynched by Hindu mobs over allegations of eating beef or smuggling cow, an animal considered holy to Hindus. Muslim businesses have been boycotted, their localities have been bulldozed, and places of worship have been set on fire. Sometimes, open calls have been made for their genocide. The hearts of Muslims continue to be broken. No Muslim opposes the construction of the Ram temple, but such unilateral changes are impacting India's culture.

The Ascendancy of BJP

The second leg of BJP's rule began to make clear their real intentions. After 2019, there was a new trend in policymaking. We saw things changing in the laws. A fundamental rule, for instance, was the Citizenship (Amendment) Act. It was passed to make religion the criterion for accessing Indian nationality. Only non-Muslim refugees from Bangladesh, Afghanistan, and Pakistan were eligible for citizenship. Also, the government passed new laws to make inter-religious marriages more difficult.

There was also the revocation of Article 370, which had granted some autonomy for Kashmir, India's only Muslim-majority state. These laws were all passed simultaneously after the 2019 election. These elections transformed a de facto ethnic democracy into a de jure ethnic democracy. But they also marked a shift toward authoritarianism. This authoritarianism took different forms.

The press in India used to be vibrant, like the judiciary. That's over. The BJP used the leverage it had on the owners. The people who own the media in India are all businessmen. And these businessmen have other businesses. They need the government's support, and if the government is not happy with some of the journalists, they ask the businesspeople to ease out the journalists.

Modi seems more prevalent across India than it has much to do with the magnitude of anti-Muslim prejudice. It is so strong. People find refuge in the BJP against Muslims and Pakistan. It has a lot to do with the public sphere. They have propagated such diabolical images of Muslims that now it's deeply rooted in the society's psyche. So, for that reason, you can say the popular support remains strong.

Modi's prime ministership symbolises, for many Indians, a civilisational resurgence on a scale not seen before. His mass appeal reflects not just a desire for better governance but also a larger shift in the Indian worldview. For Modi's supporters and Hindus in particular, Modi's meteoric rise has primarily helped in showcasing India's renewed sense of self as an ancient civilisation on the threshold of a global rebirth.

The Great Prejudice

The scale of anti-Muslim prejudice in India and how it has openly infected many areas of Indian public life, especially in the past decade, is astonishing and depressing. Why has Hinduism become such an appealing identity and Muslims such a disdained community? You can only understand it if you look at the modernisation of Indian society after 1991 when economic liberalisation resulted in more growth, urbanisation, and consumerism. These were the ingredients of a new middle class to become the core electorate of the BJP. This group became affluent but also rootless. They searched for an identity and found it in Hindu nationalism, which endowed them with cultural anchor points. This upper-caste middle class turned to new, modern, English-speaking gurus and sectarian movements in Gujarat and elsewhere. It started to follow the yoga classes of saffron-clad masters on television. The BJP has been very good at tapping that source of legitimacy by co-opting these gurus. More generally, the Ayodhya movement for building the temple in Ayodhya has enabled the BJP to capitalise on this appetite for Hinduism and pride in a Hindu identity.

Finally, they won because, in 2020, the Supreme Court of India said, go ahead, you can lay the first stone. Modi acts as though he were a priest as if he were the tremendous priestly head of India. You have a kind of theocracy in the making here, right? It explains an essential part of his popularity now that Modi is actively courting the world's gaze to felicitate his country's achievements.

BJP's International Appeal

BJP is keen to highlight the economic transformation he has presided over, making India an increasingly vital player on the world stage. And he is playing up his democratic bona fides. But a much darker narrative is starting to define Modi's India. The government has been systematically oppressing, marginalising, and inciting hatred toward its 220-million Muslim minority. This campaign has been slowly gathering momentum over the years and has reached new intensity levels today. India is not a healthy democracy.

Outside India's parliamentary edifice, several civil society groups are standing up for a pluralistic India and Muslim rights; the Supreme Court has been the most potent check on the BJP. But even among the country's highest judges, there is a sense of exasperated helplessness. "The state is impotent. The state is powerless. It does not act in time. Why do we have a state if it remains silent?" Justice KM Joseph exclaimed during a recent hearing that condemned local BJP authorities for not prosecuting hate-speech violations at rallies.

Foreign nations that buy into the P.R. blitzkrieg calling India the world's largest democracy out of commercial and geostrategic interests or lazy naivety are complicit in the accelerating decline of democratic values in India. Modi has tapped into a very deep-seated psychology among members of the diaspora who want to recover lost pride in the rise of a great civilisation that has been wronged through colonisation. No one ever bothered about the so-called Hindu identity before. Canada's people have transitioned from being normal, ordinary people to Hindu fundamentalists. India has come on the world stage. Divisions within the Indian diaspora have expressed themselves in other ways. Descendants of the historically oppressed Dalit community have led a push to ban caste discrimination, pitting them against upper-caste Hindus. Today, the balance between Canada and India has shifted. Thirty years ago, the Indian economy needed Canada. Now it's a 180-degree opposite. Canada needs India. India is the growing economic and military power, not Canada.

BJP's History Purge Overlooks the Rich Muslim Heritage

The most effective way to destroy people is to deny and obliterate their understanding of their history.

– George Orwell

Scorn for Mughal rulers, who are considered as not ancestors of Indian Muslims and only share a similar faith, is distinctive to India's Hindu nationalists, who claim Mughals destroyed Hindu culture. It has prompted Hindu nationalists to seek ownership of hundreds of historic mosques to erase everything that remotely reflects Muslim culture. The Taj Mahal is one of India's most iconic sites. But this year, millions of students across India won't delve into the Mughal Empire that constructed it. Instead, Indian students have new textbooks that have been purged of details on the nation's Muslim history, its caste discrimination, and more, in what critics say warps the country's rich history in an attempt to further Prime Minister Narendra Modi's Hindu nationalist agenda.

When Indian children began the school year this week, students in thousands of classrooms were issued new textbooks on history and politics that either watered down or purged key details from India's past that Prime Minister Narendra Modi's ruling party finds inconvenient to its Hindu nationalist vision for the country.

The Indian government has been accused of rewriting history to fit its Hindu nationalist agenda after school textbooks were edited to remove references to Mahatma Gandhi's opposition to Hindu nationalism, as well as mention of a controversial religious riot in which the prime minister, Narendra Modi, was implicated.

India's recent textbook purges show a similar disregard for history and facts, with the government seeking to alter how it was traditionally taught and cherry-pick what it wants students to learn — and what it wants to ignore. On top of the demonisation agenda is the Mughals, a dynasty that ruled parts of northern and central India during its heyday from about 1560 to 1720. Despite removing the 1400-year-long Muslim rule from textbooks, it will be impossible to destroy the forts, palaces, and cities built by the Muslims and, of course, their contribution to Indian arts, music, and cuisine. And, of course, the administrative structure to manage the massive Mughal Empire has changed very little since then and is still used today. If Indians want to document the history or censor sections of history texts, it should not be done with the sledgehammer approach as has been done.

Among the essential contents removed are chapters on the history of the Mughals, the Muslim rulers who controlled much of India between the 16th and 19th centuries. The ruling Bharatiya Janata Party (BJP), which has pursued a Hindu nationalist agenda that has moved India away from its secular foundations, has been open about its desire to rewrite the country's history and break away from what it describes as the "slave mentality" of colonial oppressors.

Historically, Muslims were pioneers in developing several branches of mathematics in South Asia, and India's most iconic landmark, the Taj Mahal, is a testament to their architectural prowess. In a time when we should be trying to build bridges between the West and Islam to address suspicions and misunderstandings, the Indian government's behaviour hinders the process. The democratic world needs Modi to showcase awareness and a strong sense of empathy. The American essayist Edward Abbey once said: "A patriot must always be ready to defend his country against his government." If Modi does not change his ways, India will need to look for such a faithful patriot.

Among the deleted passages from 12th-grade history and politics texts, Gandhi's "steadfast pursuit of Hindu-Muslim unity provoked Hindu extremists so much that they made several attempts to assassinate" him. Gandhi "was particularly disliked by those who wanted India to become a country for the Hindus, just as Pakistan was for Muslims." "Instances, like in Gujarat, alert us to the dangers of using religious sentiments for political purposes. This poses a threat to democratic politics."

Textbook Wars

A key piece of the BJP's agenda involves twisting history to demonise Muslims, and Hindu nationalists often zero in on the Mughals. Chief among Hindu nationalist disinformation about the Mughals is that these kings fuelled Hindu-Muslim conflict, a phenomenon that largely developed during British colonial rule (1757–1947). By vilifying earlier Indian kings, the British deflected attention from their exploitative and harmful colonial enterprise.

Contemporary Hindu nationalists follow British colonial ideas regarding Indian history, but they go further in attacking the Mughals. Sometimes Hindu nationalists falsely accuse the Mughals of committing genocide. Other times they falsely malign the Mughals as colonialists, which depicts them—and by extension, all Muslims today—as a foreign threat to India.

Hindu nationalists have, in turn, attacked the Taj Mahal as a Mughal-built monument, omitting it from tourist booklets and promoting the conspiracy theory that it used to be a Shiva Temple. They have removed parts of Mughal history from school textbooks. This renders many Indian children ignorant of key parts of their history, including that the Mughals built a multicultural empire, patronised Hindu and Muslim religious groups, and relied on Hindu elites known as Rajputs to rule.

Purging Brings A New History

Having gained political ascendancy, Hindutva bhakts are trying to bend historical, archaeological, and linguistic evidence to their will by appointing people to committees and academic positions based on their political orientation, irrespective of their qualifications. This process is damaging institutions of higher learning and eventually corrupting the history and science taught in schools across the nation in an attempt to raise a generation imbued with their ideology. However, before that indoctrination can proceed full-steam, the BJP must comprehensively counter the established account of India's history, which places the roots of Sanskrit and Vedic civilisation outside India's borders.

The governing party's leaders have also tried to minimise the founding fathers' arguments for why India's diversity could survive only under a secular umbrella, co-opting the legacy of many lay leaders as they push to remake India into a Hindu-first nation. The purge of books on Indian Muslims and the vandalisation of monuments are also part of a broader campaign to undermine the community and its rich history. The Taj Mahal is an iconic 17th-century mausoleum built by another Mughal emperor, Shah Jahan, but Modi's deputies frequently disparage it in remarks.

The obliteration of India's Islamic history and culture is also reflected in rewriting school textbooks in provinces ruled by the BJP. Mughal rulers such as Akbar and Shah Jahan, who embellished

India's cultural legacy, are being reintroduced in academia as debauched, villainous invaders who robbed India of its Hindu heritage. The cuts are wide-ranging. Chapters on the country's historic Islamic rulers are either slimmed down or gone; an entire chapter in the 12th-grade history textbook, "Kings and Chronicles: The Mughal Courts," was deleted. The books omit references to the 2002 riots in the Indian state of Gujarat, where hundreds of Indian Muslims were killed while Modi was the state's leader. Details on India's caste system, caste discrimination, and minority communities are missing.

The infamous book, *The History of India*, as 'told by its historians', has done the most incredible damage to Muslim history authored by Elliot and Dawson. There was a time when this book was widely prescribed in schools and colleges. A casual glance at a few pages would reveal the authors' determined effort to poison readers' minds against Muslim rulers. The authors, keen to contrast what they understood as the justice and efficiency of British rule with the so-called cruelty and despotism of the Muslim rulers who had preceded that rule, were anything but sympathetic to the "Muhammadan" period of Indian history. Today's politics in India's history textbooks promote communal strife by creating a historical consciousness that gives pride of place to religion and proposes a narrative that traces back community identities and antagonisms and legitimises their existence. Several new studies from Western scholarship also show that the Mughals were pluralists and catholic in their outlook and policies.

A Time to Heal

The present government's interest in this historical course correction is not new. There has always been a school of thought ideologically opposed to the conventional understanding of how medieval kings ruled. Followers of this school of thought question the sources suggesting that medieval Muslim kings and royals often struck alliances with their Hindu counterparts.

Textbooks have been quietly edited to remove meaningful chunks of history from India's Mughal era, including the achievements of that Muslim dynasty, even though their legacy lives on in iconic architecture, cultural traditions, and so much more. References to independent India's first education minister, Maulana Abul Kalam Azad — a senior figure in the country's struggle for freedom from British rule, a close comrade of Mahatma Gandhi, and a beacon of Hindu-Muslim unity — have also been purged.

Yet the intelligentsia in India has barely registered even a whimper of protest over this brazen bulldozing of history. This is no less than lying to students. It hurts academic scholarship and access to the most basic facts for future generations. The medieval historical period is such a crucial era of India's past — one when the country's economy might have reached its peak, among other achievements — and excluding it from the curriculum would amount to gross intellectual dishonesty. Historical narratives are always open to alternate views, revision, debate, and healthy discussion, but omitting facts is an unacademic approach.

Perhaps more than the harm to historical academic scholarship, these deletions can be conceived as a message to Indian minorities. By obliterating essential parts of India's Muslim past from textbooks, the government seems to give in to those who believe that the country's history and future belong only to Hindus.

Akbar's Unique Experiences

According to Audrey Truschke, a well-known modern historian,much of the current religious conflict in India has been fuelled by ideological assumptions about that period rather than an accurate rendering of the subcontinent's history. In her book, *Culture of Encounters: Sanskrit at the Mughal Court,* Truschke says that the heyday of Muslim rule in India from the 16th to 18th centuries was, in fact, one of "tremendous cross-cultural respect and fertilisation," not religious or cultural conflict.

A leading scholar of South Asian cultural and intellectual history, Truschke argues that this more divisive interpretation developed during the colonial period from 1757 to 1947. "The British benefited from pitting Hindus and Muslims against one another and portrayed themselves as neutral saviours who could keep ancient religious conflicts at bay," she says. "While colonialism ended in the 1940s, the modern Hindu right has found tremendous political value in continuing to proclaim and create endemic Hindu-Muslim conflict." Meanwhile, it is a welcome development that the Supreme Court has ended the name-changing spree of cities and their streets. While dismissing a petition which sought directions to restore the names of places changed by "foreign barbaric invaders," the Supreme Court said, "A country cannot remain a prisoner of the past."

Biased Historians

The tragedy, however, is that historians have not documented the entire history without bias. These historians were motivated by resentment against Muslims and were more loyal to their ideology than facts. Zealot rulers patronised them. Several ideology-minded scholars, even among intellectuals, courted the rulers by destroying and dismantling anything Islamic. So much so that chauvinists appropriated Islamic architecture and Hindu ideologies. In several cases, the rulers actively patronised the rewriting of history to suit their ideology.

The most significant challenge for authentic historians is to resurrect Islamic heritage and purge them of alien accretions. One brave and passionate historian who has taken upon this audacious task is Syed Ubaidur Rahman, whose zeal and passion for this mission are admirable. Rahman has culled a vast corpus of unique insights from the humongous mountain of history and condensed them in such an incredible style that the book's conciseness keeps the reader engrossed and helps him understand medieval history in its proper perspective.

Hindu nationalist ideologues still periodically subject Indian Muslims to loyalty tests. As the great British statesman James Baldwin writes in Notes of a Native Son: "People are trapped in history, and history is trapped in them." A reappraisal of history can alone put the record straight and clear the misconceptions created by partisan historians, in whose works fantasy, conjecture, and stereotypes have replaced fact and reality. Or else we will confirm the fears of the great thinker, Walter Benjamin: "The victors write history." The paradox underlying this puzzle has been written with rare clarity in the dedication template of Bhagwan S. Gidwani, author of 'The Sword of Tipu Sultan', who devoted 13 years to part-time research on his book in the archives of half a dozen countries for writing his novel. It reads: "To the country which lacks a historian; to men whom history owes rehabilitation."

Efforts are afoot to rewrite the Indian history of the recent past. Muslims need to make conscious efforts to preserve their account. It is not an easy job and requires resources and determination. Muslim organisations must take the lead or support those filling the gap in their ways.

The issue of renaming places has been prominent in public discussions for quite some time now. This case rested on the argument that many monuments are named after "looters" who came from abroad. However, the two-judge bench of Justice K M Joseph and Justice B V Nagarathna said that one cannot revisit history selectively and that there is no space for bigotry in Hinduism.

Muslim Future in the Indian Homeland

Constitutions were made for modern democratic societies, just as scriptures were created in pre-modern traditional societies. However, while everyone had a clear idea of how the ancient religious texts worked for everyone in the older societies, few people have a clear idea of how the Constitution can work for the marginalised. Only the executive, legislature, and judiciary respect the spirit that animates it.

The Conflict Between Islam and Modernity

When Pakistan finally adopted a Constitution, almost nine years after the Partition, it endorsed Islam as the state religion. The promise of a pluralist India, as envisaged by the country's founders, prevailed over the warnings of the pro-Partition Muslim League (which went on to become the party of Pakistan's founders) and the Muslim minority, which believed they would be subordinate to the Hindu majority, decided to migrate to Pakistan. However, there was a substantial majority of Muslims who believed in a secular credo and had faith in leaders who promised equality for all, and they chose India as the country of their settlement.

It is an admirable feat that the Constitution offers remedies even to the most marginalised people in society, and equally commendable is the fact that these people place enough trust and confidence in the Constitution that they turn to the courts seeking to enforce their rights. Other faiths were accorded equal status.

Islam, unlike Marxism, continues to be deeply rooted and present in everyday life, profoundly influencing various societies and ideologies. It is robust enough to survive the complexities that have buffeted world civilisations in the past and has answers even for potential threats hovering around in the social environment.

Constitutions were made for modern democratic societies, much like how scriptures were composed in pre-modern traditional societies. However, while there was a clear understanding of how ancient religious texts functioned for everyone in the older societies, few people have a clear idea of how the Constitution can work for the marginalised. Only the executive, legislature, and judiciary respect the spirit that animates it.

While Pakistan nears economic collapse, Indian fantasies of becoming a superpower lie shattered amid shrivelled growth and ecological calamity. Violence and brutality were hardly unknown in India: cities were sacked, massacres and rapes were perpetrated on ordinary people, and places of worship were desecrated. Yet it would be a mistake to view the parched presence of India and Pakistan as evidence of progress in history. Muslims continue to suffer significant political, social, and economic deprivation. Their situation is so dire that economic reforms take precedence over all other amelioration policies. Improvements in their social and educational conditions, as well as the much-talked-about gender reforms, will automatically follow their economic uplift.

They lag on almost every measure of success — the number of Muslims in the IAS, the police, and the army, the number of Muslim-owned companies in the top five hundred Indian firms, and the percentage of Muslim CEOs or national newspaper editors are far behind their statistical entitlements. And then, millions of Muslims live in abject poverty.

The backwardness of Muslims deprives the country of nearly one-fifth of its valuable talent. Economic problems cannot be solved with civil rights remedies but can be relieved with public and private actions encouraging economic redevelopment. The government has aggressively been pursuing the agenda of reforms in the personal laws of Muslims, alleging genuine concern for Muslim women. However, economic backwardness is a much more complex and bitter reality for Muslim Indians. The state can't turn its eyes away, especially when focusing many telescopes on the community's social issues.

It amounts to questioning the purity of the nationalism of Muslims, in the same way the so-called upper castes have questioned the purity of the spiritualism of the so-called backward castes. But Indian Muslims have neither compromised nationalism nor abandoned religion. India is depriving itself of one-fifth of its valuable talents by keeping Muslims backwards. Economic problems cannot be solved with civil rights remedies but could be relieved with public and private actions encouraging economic redevelopment.

The Sanctity of Pluralism

Life in a plural age should be welcomed because we can pursue our paths and learn from others. It's not that simple, of course. In truth, this is the most demanding form of pluralism. It means that I must take responsibility for my commitments and do so in a particular way: by recognising that they are commitments others do not share.

At the same time, this diversity safeguards our humanity. If everyone were to follow the same path, if utopia were found, then there would be no more questions, no more questing, only subsistence living. It's often forgotten that Thomas More's "utopia" coinage means "no place." A philosophy of pluralism, though, represents a real place because of the grit of others. Others protect my humanity;

their truth sustains my truth, and their difference enhances my singularity. Ramadan continues.

But perhaps the most challenging characteristic of this version of pluralism is that it is not so much a political philosophy as a philosophy of life. At its heart, it relies on the individual and how we will be with others.

The political idea of pluralism is often limited to where people can tolerably exist based on various groups and beliefs. But we need to go much beyond this threshold. There are divergent strands in public discourse that must be recognised and harmonised. We may argue, or we may disagree. But we cannot deny the actual prevalence of a diversity of opinions. The plurality of our society has come through the assimilation of ideas over centuries. Secularism and inclusion are a matter of faith for us. It is our composite culture that makes us one nation.

We have to rethink the very ideas of Islam and modernity to end the confusion caused by the controversial or ideological use of the terms, which portrays them as two antagonistic forces. Muslims are India's most significant religious minority. Muslims have considered India their home for more than a millennium. They have become so seamlessly integrated into its social mainstream that several strands of their culture and tradition have become part of the national fabric. But the tragedy is that Muslims are so marginalised that their presence in critical public spheres is almost invisible. Most of them are poor, semi-literate, and forced into ghettos.

The demonisation of social groups through bigoted policies and holding them responsible for all national ills has become a favourite narrative. This script has repeatedly played itself out in history with disastrous consequences. Fundamentally, the state is trying to reconfigure the concept of Indian identity to make it synonymous with being Hindu. The right-wing is attempting to dismantle India's secular traditions and turn the country into a religious state as a homeland for Hindus. Muslims can see a shadow world creeping upon them. This dangerous game will tear apart the diverse, delicate social fabric that has existed in India for ages. India's founders advocated an Indian brand of secularism designed to hold the country's disparate communities together under one roof. Indeed, Jawaharlal Nehru pronounced India's composite culture as one of its greatest strengths.

Indian secularism is the by-product of an entire civilisation. According to the famous novelist and member of the Nehru family, Nayantara Sahgal, "We are unique in the world because so many cultures and religions enrich us. Now, they want to squash us into one culture. So it is a difficult time. We do not want to lose our richness. We do not want to lose anything. All that Islam has brought us, what Christianity has brought us, what Sikhism has brought us. Why should we lose all this? We are not all Hindus, but we are all Hindustani."

The BJP has a history of using religious fault lines as a political tool to expand its constituency. Hindu or Hindutva chauvinism continues to drive India dangerously away from its pluralistic moorings. It is trying to recast the story of India from that of a secular democracy accommodating a uniquely diverse population to that of a Hindu nation dominating its minorities, especially the country's Muslims. The core philosophy rests on a combustible idea: that only followers of the so-called Indic religions (which it will define) can genuinely be Indians. These regressive policies are seeding long-term domestic instability, undermining interfaith harmony, and tarnishing India's reputation for peaceful coexistence. The BJP government at the centre and in the states keep targeting Muslims with incendiary messages, encouraging and emboldening vigilante violence against them. Such violence is typically followed by state inaction and apparent bias.

The Despondency of Muslims

The most apt description of a communal frenzy — and we had hundreds of them — came from Justice Madon, who enquired about the infamous Bhiwandi riots. Summing up his report for the Maharashtra government after the riots in Bhiwandi and Jalgaon in 1970, Justice Dinshah P. Madon wrote, "It was a lonely, arduous, and weary journey through a land of hatred and violence, prejudice and perjury. The encounters on the way were with men without compassion, lusting for the blood of their fellow men, with politicians who trafficked in communal hatred and religious fanaticism, with local leaders who sought power by sowing disunity and bitterness, with police officers and policemen who were unworthy of their uniform, with investigating officers without honour and scruples, with men committed to falsehood and wedded to fraud and with dealers in mayhem and murder."

Muslims have traditionally been craftsmen, and most craft skills have been overtaken by mechanisation, rendering most artisans' skills obsolete under the prevailing political economy. These people have lost their traditional livelihoods and cannot regain them in export markets, for instance, without government and business support. On the contrary, Hindu traders and businesspeople have prospered from the country's booming economic growth.

The mood among India's Muslims is bleak, and they perceive their position as steadily undermined by the new "nationalism" gripping the country. Indian Muslims are facing more pressing issues. Various surveys have highlighted their poor economic and social conditions.

Modi earned a reputation for economic management in his home state of Gujarat and was elected on a platform of rejuvenating Indian growth and income. Yet hopes for business-friendly reform have come to little, and the economy has been slowing since mid-2018. The prime minister still has a choice: to continue down the path of pursuing divisive religious politics to reshape India into an even more overtly Hindu state or, instead, focus on growth and genuine reform. Not temples, but modern infrastructure, a buoyant economy, communal harmony, employment for most people, and opportunities to rise out of poverty would be the true tonic to heal India's civilisational wounds.

Islam Needs Renewal, Not Reforms

In recent years, clichéd calls for reform of Islam have acquired more stringent tones: "We need a Muslim reformation." "Islam needs reformation from within." Such headlines keep flashing in the media. Yet, if Muslims are true to themselves and their scriptures, Islam doesn't need a reformation. Muslims need to save themselves from intolerance and dogmatism.

The vision of some reformers asks Muslims to abandon 14 hundred years of accepted dogma in favour of a radical and demanding new methodology that would set them free from the burdens of traditional jurisprudence. In recent years, an enormous industry of reform-minded interpreters has arisen to explain, contextualise, downplay, or ignore them, often quoting the well-known verse that says there is "no compulsion in religion."

Islam is worlds apart from Christianity. The two faiths aren't analogous, and it is deeply ignorant to try and impose a neatly linear, Eurocentric view of history on diverse Muslim-majority countries in Asia or Africa. Each religion has its dissent and culturally evolved through uniquely distinct traditional paths, and each religion's followers have been affected by geopolitics and socio-economic processes in myriad ways. The theologies of Islam and Christianity are far apart: the former, for instance, has never had a Catholic-style clerical class answering to a divinely appointed pope. The truth is that Islam has already had its reformation, in the sense of stripping cultural accretions and a process of supposed "purification."

The truth is that Islam has already reformed in the sense of stripping cultural accretions and a process of supposed "purification." Wasn't reform precisely what was offered to the masses of the Hijaz by Muhammad Ibn Abdul Wahhab, the mid-18th century itinerant preacher? He provided an austere Islam cleansed of what he believed to be innovations, which eschewed centuries of mainstream scholarship and commentary. He rejected the authority of the traditional ulema or religious leaders.

The idea of the reformation of Islam can be better understood if we explore how close Wahhabism is to Protestantism or Catholicism is highly complex and paradoxical. In Islam, there has always been the argument that Wahhabism arose directly as an imitation of Protestant Christianity. And some Wahhabis do make this comparison. They say, "We are creating a Protestant Islam." But many Catholics respond to this by saying to Wahhabis, "If you're looking for models from the Christian world, the Catholics are much better models.

There is one significant difference, however. Protestantism did not attempt to enforce conformity. Protestantism fostered pluralism. Wahhabism does not promote pluralism, unlike traditional Islam, which is pluralistic and non-conformist and allows for diverse opinions. And that's why, in the end, I now essentially reject the parallel.

Abd al-Wahhab was the most significant reformist who believed that Islam had been corrupted and weakened by the Ottomans and needed to return to its roots. But his brand of an original, authentic Islam was harsher and more stripped down than the religion that the Prophet Muhammad had founded centuries before. Al-Wahhab forbade many practices and traditions that were an established part of Muslim culture, such as the celebration of the Prophet's birthday, the decoration of mosques, and the use of music in worship and daily life.

People must realise that Wahhabism embodies violence because Wahhabism begins by saying that everybody who isn't a Wahhabi who calls himself a Muslim isn't a Muslim. And that is, in essence, a violent proposition. Some Wahhabis are not directly involved in going off and killing people, but they support the ideology that supports the people who are going off and killing people. The difference is that the Wahhabis have a religious dispensation that creates a totalistic sense of self-righteousness. Nazism and Stalinism didn't have this.

Renewal and Reform

Renewal and reform are the essential components of the new learning methodology of the Qur'an. The Salafis lead the most influential movement in this direction. They signify a stripping away of accumulated misreading and wrong or lapsed practices, as in the Protestant Reformation, and a return to the founding texts of the Qur'an and the Sunna—guidelines based on the recorded words and deeds of the Prophet.

Nearly a century after it emerged in Egypt, political Islam is redefining the Muslim world. Also called Islamism, this potent ideology holds that the billion-strong global Muslim community would be free and great if only it were pious—that is, if Muslims lived under state-enforced Islamic law, or Shar'ia, as they have done for most of Islamic history. Islamists have long been confronted by Muslims who reject Shar'ia and non-Muslims who try to get them to reject it.

Salafism, imported into Egypt from Saudi Arabia and publicised around the world thanks to petrodollars, is the enemy of anything moderate and tolerant. The Salafis believe that the only true path is to follow the practices of the early generations of Muslims – literally.

Although most Egyptians do not identify as Salafis, their thinking has been greatly influenced by Salafism, especially the younger generation. Much effort is expended in public displays of religiosity, such as beards, prayer beads, prayer calluses, and women's clothing. At the same time, the spiritual aspect of religion and the proper ethics Muslims should adhere to take a back seat.

Reforms are, of course, needed across the crisis-ridden Muslimmajority world: political, socio-economic, and, yes, religious too. Muslims need to rediscover their heritage of pluralism, tolerance, and mutual respect – embodied in the Prophet's letter to the monks of St Catherine's monastery or the "Convivencia" (or coexistence) of medieval Muslim Spain.

Responding to those who claim that Shar'ia fuels much of the violence and political instability in Muslim countries, several scholars argue that Islamic law is the key to rebuilding the political order in the country. They point out that Shar'ia is invoked to justify misogyny and human rights abuses, but that it has also been. It is not Shar'ia but struggles over the legal system that has been the primary source of contention and conflict going back to the beginning of the colonial era. We must try to understand how successive national states grappled with integrating Western jurisprudence, customary law, and Shar'ia.

WE cannot judge the era of the founding of Islam by the values of our own time: and, indeed, what we understand as the emancipation of women was never really considered by any of the great monotheistic religions. Some of the West's Christian establishments have accepted relatively equal rights, abortion and divorce only under pressure from women's associations and after long battles. Islam is aware of these changes. It is inclined to blame the commentators of the Qur'an or canon law for the prevailing repression of women.

Westerners think of Islamic societies as backwards-looking, inhumanely governed, and oppressed by religion, comparing them to their enlightened, secular democracies. However, measuring the cultural distance between the West and Islam is a complex undertaking, and the reality is that the distance is narrower than they assume. Islam is not just a religion, and indeed not just a fundamentalist political movement. It is a civilisation and a way of life that varies from one Muslim country to another but is animated by a common spirit far more humane than most Westerners realise.

Repression of Women

How did a religion that initially offered women greater freedom than they had known in traditional societies come to be associated with their repression? Muslim feminists have begun to reclaim the independence and respect accorded to women during the early centuries of Islam. The problem is less religion itself than the way commentators have interpreted it. The Qur'an has multiple teachings with many meanings, and Muslims have always been free to comment on them according to circumstances. The texts have been interpreted over centuries to endorse conservatism and intolerance and promote openness, freedom, forgiveness, and intellectual revival.

There is plenty of historical evidence for the servitude of women and the contempt and hatred they have suffered. Women's inequitable legal and social situation in most Muslim countries is deplorable. But is this situation directly attributable to a religion that is seen as sexist, or is it the result of religious or civil authorities interpreting that religion according to a male desire to dominate, despite Islam's insistence on equality?

Unlike Christianity, Islam was concerned with politics and governance from the start. The Muslim rule that developed in the lifetime of the Prophet required attention to principles of community life, justice, administration, relations with non-Muslims, defence, and foreign policy. The main new ideas were a vision of what constitutes good governance, law, and a just society. The Prophet came not to protect the status quo but to reform and change. Women, for instance, were given legal status (where they had none before) and concrete legal protection within society.

If Prophet Muhammad's life were revolutionary, its aftermath would have seen a monological recital of Hadiths and inflexible analyses of Qur'anic verses, where historical context is taken up or ignored to suit the interpreter. Memories of early Islam have hardened into dogma, and many scholars have taken the Hadiths as stone tablets.

Islam received the unique stamp of Prophet Mohammed's success. Unlike earlier prophets, Prophet Muhammad lived for some years as the head of a state of his creation and to which he gave laws. He shaped laws about marriage, inheritance, divorce, and similar matters, aiming to reform generally recognised customs. He restricted the number of wives a man might have to four—imposed an almost impossible fulfilment of a condition that equality is maintained among them. Women had no inheritance rights; the new code granted them the request for half of the men's share. Slavery was widespread; Islam outlawed it except for captives taken in war, and for these, it introduced reforms and ways of regaining freedom. Wine drinking was gradually controlled, and usury was forbidden. The caste system, which was still in vogue, was abolished, as was the cruel practice of burying unwanted female babies alive.

We need to understand every religion from its primary scriptures and not from secondary sources, which are unfortunately prone to many interpretations that may be erroneous or deceptive and are usually representative of a particular school of thought. The only lasting solution will be to liberate society from manmade religion and return to the pristine message of the scriptures. These scriptures had a simple, straightforward, and plain-speaking message for all humanity, which got distorted at the hands of the modern tools of intellectual sophistry and sterile polemics. We need to sanitise our bodies, environment, minds, and intellect.

The great modern reformist thinker Fazlur Rahman firmly believed that one of the primary purposes of the Qurʿān was to create a justice-based society. He saw the Prophet Muhammad as a social reformist who sought to empower the poor, the weak, and the vulnerable. He viewed the Qurʿān as a source from which ethical principles could be derived rather than a book of laws.

He played the role of father, husband, chief, warrior, friend, and Prophet. His respect for learning, tolerance of others, generosity of spirit, concern for the weak, gentle piety, and desire for a better, cleaner world would constitute the main elements of the Muslim ideal. For Muslims, the life of the Prophet is the triumph of hope over despair and light over darkness. For instance, Rahman argues that the practice of family law in Islamic history had not accorded females the equal rights to which they appear to be entitled based on the Prophet's example and teachings of the Qurʿān.

Earlier attempts were made to create new ideologies promising rejuvenation. Jamal al-Din al-Afghani and Muhammad Abdouh led attempts to make Islam more legible by calling for adapting Muslim life to the West's views on economic and political modernity. They never called themselves Salafists (for them, it was about returning to the sources to find compatibility with these new challenges).

The Discourse of Fazlur Rahman

The acclaimed modernist scholar Fazlur Rahman writes in his book *Islam and Modernity*: "A historical critique of theological developments in Islam is the first step toward a reconstruction of Islamic theology. This critique should reveal the extent of the dislocation between the world view of the Qur'an and various schools of theological speculation in Islam and point the way toward a new theology." This is a significant suggestion that should have been considered seriously and would have benefited the Islamic world immensely. For him, it was the intellectual ossification and replacement of scholarship based on original thought by one based on commentaries and super-commentaries, the closing of the gate of ijtihad, and the establishment of the Islamic method solely on taqlid (blind imitation) which led to the decline.

Fazlur Rahman's goal was to reassess the Islamic intellectual tradition and provide a way forward for Muslims. In his view, re-examining Islamic methodology in the light of the Qur'an was a prerequisite for any reform in Islamic thought.

Rahman says, "Muslim scholars have never attempted ethics of the Qur'an, systematically or otherwise. Yet no one who has studied the Qur'an carefully can fail to be impressed by its moral fervour. Its ethics, indeed, are its essence and are also the vital link between theology and law. The Qur'an tends to concretise the ethical, clothe the general in a particular paradigm, and translate the ethical into legal or quasi-legal commands. But it is precisely the sign of its moral fervour that is not content only with generalisable ethical propositions but is keen on translating them into existing paradigms. However, the Qur'an always explains the objectives or principles that are the essence of its laws."

At the same time, there needs to be abundant caution. Reform is an unruly horse that can go berserk unless adequately saddled. In several societies, the hardliners have served as vigilantes and sentinels of their faith. Their resistance has helped winnow the weaker strands in the formulation of new trajectories of thought and discourse. The bigoted and intolerant forces can acquire aggressive postures to suit their distorted understanding and ideological positions. Akbar is considered a great liberal king. However, we must not forget that he made extraordinary efforts to subvert Islam by attempting to reinvent the faith.

Shaykh Ahmad Sirhindī, the great mystic and theologian, was primarily responsible for the reassertion and revival of orthodox Sunnite Islam as a reaction against the syncretistic tendencies promoted by Akbar. It was a serious attempt to dilute Islam and reinterpret its original philosophy. Persecuted for his outspokenness and straightforwardness, he is today revered as a saint and saviour of Islam. Similarly, Dara Shikoh was not just a great liberalist of his time but was charged with blasphemy by clerics. Both Akbar and Dara Shikoh were secular individuals. Still, their creative efforts had much to do with power and politics. Nothing by way of communal harmony and interfaith cordiality eroded some of Islam's most cherished values and traditions.

The Place of Hardliners

Hardliners have their unique place in all discourses, and their presence helps redefine unchecked and anarchic impulses. Always delay judgement no matter who you are, how experienced, and how knowledgeable you are. Give others the privilege to explain themselves. What you see may not be the reality. Never conclude for others. This is why we should never focus only on the surface and judge others without fully understanding their perspective. This requires an enormous amount of tolerance.

All scriptures are, above all, a spiritual and moral resource that, if they are correctly understood and internalised both in letter and spirit, provide the reader with helpful guidance through the complexities of modern life. It is the nature of the human dialogue that finally culminates in the direction one is seeking for their salvation. Human perversity and ignorance can turn this overtly benevolent and benign exercise into intricate, complicated means to divide people. Instead of divine consciousness and guidance being the moral principles that bring people together, they become the embodiment of the most fundamental differences. They should be seen as a training manual for human nature. Submitting ourselves to their wisdom should mean testing and interrogating all our ideas and experiences afresh in the light of the fresh dose of thinking ingrained during the dialogue. We must all teach ourselves to read these divine and holy books liberated from the weight of tradition and classical commentaries. The real wisdom that we can glean from them is the one that ignites our spirituality when we constantly think outside the box of our earthly concerns by keeping in mind the intersection of time and timelessness.

While several reformist thinkers continued their creative work in the last two centuries, it was the great poet Muhammad Iqbal. He conceived a very coherent and inspiring philosophy that crystallised around Islamic ideals. His Islam is not the Islam of primitive punishments, the veil, and bigoted mullahs, but the Islam which provided a new light of thought and learning to the world and of heroic action and glorious deeds. He was devoted to the Prophet and believed in his message. Iqbal regarded as 'nullification' the search for 'inner meanings' or 'hidden meanings' in either the code of Muhammad (peace be upon him) or in his way of life, which he found not only satisfying but also convincing. He blamed the Persian poets for confusing the message of Islam. As he put it, "The Persian poets tried to undermine the way of Islam by a very roundabout, though apparently heart–alluring, manner. They denounced every good thing of Islam and made contemplation in a monastery the highest crusade in the way of God."

Iqbal preached action. He was a rebel against all the accretions that had gathered around Islam due to Hellenic and Persian influences and wanted to cleanse it so that the world could, once again, witness the glory of Islam in its pristine form. For the laziness and lethargy that had gripped the Islamic fold, Iqbal blamed the Sufis. They, with their Iranian background and Greek ideas, had corrupted the religion of Muhammad (peace be upon him). As Iqbal explains, "It is surprising that the poetry of Sufism in Islam was produced during the period of political decline. The nation which exhausts its fund of energy and power, as was the case with the Muslims after the Tartar invasions, changes the outlook. Weakness becomes an object of beauty and appreciation, and resignation from the world is a source of satisfaction."

Iqbal's poems reflect the pain and agony he felt at the degeneration of Islam. This feeling is patent in every couplet. Muslims are repeatedly asked to go back to the early era of Islam when the spirit of Muhammad (peace be upon him) goaded his followers to conquer half the world and brought enlightenment to people of various regions and colours. While Iqbal retained his admiration for the otherworldliness of Sufi mystics, he rejected their belief in the world's transitoriness and the unreality of life. He was appalled by Western commercialism and greed, lamented the loss of the Muslim empire, and was saddened by the decadence of Islam.

A legacy can be preserved only if it is honoured and respected by its custodians. We must try to understand and delineate those attributes that aided the personalities of yesteryears to attain those levels of glory. At the same time, we have to examine the social and cultural factors that enabled them to use their talents to their farthest value and harness their energies toward the goals fruitfully. Some Muslim countries have seen the emergence of leading politicians who have unfortunately not been able to live up to the ideals of the early women and have done significant damage to the reputation of an Islamic female.

Islam is at a crossroads today, and Muslims are poised at a critical juncture in their history. The stagnation in Islamic thought is evident in the couplets of Muhammad Iqbal:

You are one people. You share in common your weal and woe.
You have one faith, one creed and to one Prophet Allegiance owe.
You have one sacred Ka'aba, one God and one holy book, the Qur'an.
Was it so difficult to unite in one community every single Mussalman?

Muslim Future in Pluralist India

"The Constitution is not for the exclusive benefit of governments and states; it also exists for the common man, the poor and the humble ... for the butcher, the baker and the candlestick maker."

These words of Justice Vivian Bose effectively sum up the entire piece of work. The book's premise challenges the (erroneous) notion that some carry: that the Constitution of India is a document for the elite and the well-off.

Constitutions were made for modern democratic societies in the same way the scriptures were made for pre-modern traditional societies. But, while everyone had a clear idea of how the ancient religious texts worked for everyone in the older societies, few people have a clear idea of how the Constitution can work for the only executive and judiciary respect that animates it. It is an appreciable feat that the Constitution offers remedies even to the most marginalised people in society, and equally commendable is the fact that these people put enough trust and confidence in the Constitution that they move the courts seeking to enforce their rights.

Other faiths were accorded equal status. Islam, unlike Marxism, continues to be deeply rooted and still present in everyday life and profoundly influences various societies and ideologies. Islam remains a system of values by which Muslims live. It is robust enough to survive the complexities that have buffeted world civilisations in the past and has the answer to even those potential threats hovering around in the social environment. Therefore, life in a plural age should be welcomed because we can pursue paths and learn from other approaches. Only, it's not that simple, of course. And in truth, this is the most demanding form of pluralism. It means that I must take responsibility for my commitments in a particular way, recognising that they are commitments others do not share. At the same time, this diversity safeguards our humanity. If everyone were to follow the same path, if utopia were found, then there would be no more questions, no more questing, only subsistence living. It's often forgotten that Thomas Moore's "utopia" coinage means "no place". A philosophy of pluralism, though, represents a real place because of the grit of others. Others protect my humanity; their truth sustains my truth, and their difference enhances my singularity. Ramadan continues.

We have to rethink the very ideas of Islam and modernity to end the confusion caused by the controversial or ideological use of the terms, which makes them two antagonistic forces. Muslims are India's most significant religious minority. Muslims have considered India their home for more than a millennium. They have become so seamlessly integrated into its social mainstream that several strands of their culture and tradition have been subsumed into the national fabric. But the tragedy is that Muslims are so marginalised that their presence in critical public spheres is almost invisible. Most of them are poor, semi-literate, and driven into ghettos.

When the British withdrew from the Indian subcontinent in 1947, paving the way for the independence of the newly partitioned nations of India and Pakistan, the Muslims could stay back in their homeland or migrate. They could resettle in Pakistan, where they would be among a Muslim majority, or remain in India, where they would live as a minority in a majority-Hindu but constitutionally secular state. However, logistically, this could never be feasible, and the problem got rooted in this vortex.

Long before the British conquered India, the Hindus had resented their Muslim Mogul masters and those who, by conversion, followed the same faith. The Muslim had all the scorn of the warrior for those less martial than himself and was politically more astute than the others. This historical background would have required more courage, tolerance, and statecraft than any leaders in India or Pakistan have yet shown to heal the hereditary strains between the two great communal factions. Seventy-five years later, those warnings have gained a new prescience. Nominally, India remains a secular state and a multipath democracy. Religious minorities account for roughly 20 per cent of the country's 1.4 billion people, including about 200 million Muslims and 28 million Christians.

However, in the last decade of rule, the inner fabric of the state has frayed. Beneath the country's apparent inclusivity runs an undercurrent of Hindu nationalism that has gained strength during the eight-year rule of Prime Minister Narendra Modi. The concern shared by many among the country's religious minorities, as well as by more secular-minded liberals within the Hindu majority, is that the country's secular and inclusive ethos is already beyond healing.

In the past, these clashes, sometimes deadlier, were usually set off by a local issue and would remain restricted to a single area. The recent waves of violence, the most widespread communal tensions in recent years, played out across several states, with multiple clashes having the uniform characteristic of one-sided punishments. They are rooted in the rhetoric of right-wing groups at the national level that are targeting Muslims through provocative campaigns emboldened by the silence of the country's top leaders. The concern, say analysts, activists, and former civil servants, is that the clashes will become more frequent, pushing the nation into a cycle of violence and instability.

These provocations by right-wing activists, which spread swiftly through social media, inspire local groups, who are increasingly turning religious occasions into political conflagrations promoting a Hindu-first vision of India that jeopardises even the basic rights of minorities, leaving apart their economic lives. When the recent tensions spilt into violence, authorities in those places rushed to dole out punishment that fell disproportionately on Muslims and in ways that circumvented the legal process.

Siege of Secularism

One of the difficulties, ideologically, is that we have rejected the global notion of secularism. The word secularism, as used by Nehru, was that religion would be excluded from the state, as it was in the French Revolution. The term was not used then, but the phenomenon was there. It was first used by (George Jacob) Holyoake (in 1851), who said secularism is morality without religion, without any idea of the afterlife. He also said secularism is linked to the idea of welfare (of people). This is the correct notion of secularism.

However, according to Dr Sarvepalli Radhakrishnan, India's second President, the idea of secularism opens the door to majority communalism. It says all religions must be tolerated, which should be, but it also says religion can't be separated from the state. There is nothing like an abstract religion. It is absurd to say that if we treat all religions equally, then religion can play a part in the state. Since there is no abstract religion, then only the majority religion can play a part.

This idea was upheld by the Supreme Court, which said instructions in religions should be there in all schools, even though the Constitution prohibits religious instructions in (government) schools. The judgement said it has to be allowed because all morality comes from saints and seers. This is historically a false statement. The saints didn't know about (social and economic) equality or gender equality. This kind of secularism is wrong. The global idea of secularism should have been upheld.

A nation is how we construct it; a nation is not a natural thing. You create a sense of (national) community and within it, little communities. If we promote sectional divisions or regional divisions, to that extent, the nation is weakened or affected adversely. So a nation has to be built up. One of the most important ways of sustaining the nation is secularism and democracy, paying attention to different regions and meeting their needs. The problem with the present government is that it lacks inclusiveness, which is necessary for the construction of a nation. So they may shout they are nationalists, but they are undermining the nation.

Today, many Hindu nationalists seem to see it as their life's mission to deprive Indian Muslims of equal rights or even expel them. They would also like to introduce Hindu religious writing into Indian law. It's important to remember that Muslims are India's largest minority, over 14 per cent of the population. There was a time when Hindus and Muslims, including my family, fought for freedom against British colonial rule. They firmly rejected the theory, propagated by power-hungry politicians, that Hindus and Muslims cannot live together in one country. Today, to suggest that Indian Muslims are anti-national and aliens, as some do, is preposterous.

Muslims in India continue to suffer significant political, social, and economic deprivation. Their situation is so dire that economic reforms precede all other amelioration policies. Improvement in their social and educational conditions, as well as the much-talked-about gender reforms, will automatically follow their economic uplift. Muslims in India are not just humiliated on the streets. They are being demonised and vilified on the big screen.

Modi has two languages: speaking eloquently and inclusively of Gandhi and democracy when the world is watching and another language of silence as his country descends into violent, Hindunationalistmajoritarianism. I have closely followed Modi and his political style over the last 15 years, and the most striking feature is what you might term the art of looking away. But what they lag on almost every measure of success — the number of Muslims in the IAS, the police and the army, the number of Muslim-owned companies in the top five hundred Indian firms, and the percentage of Muslim C.E.O.s or national newspaper editors far behind their statistical entitlements. And then millions of Muslims live in abject poverty.

Strategic Secularism

The backwardness of Muslims deprives the country of nearly one-fifth of its valuable talent. Economic problems cannot be solved with civil rights remedies but can be relieved with public and private action encouraging economic redevelopment. The government has aggressively been pursuing the agenda of reforms in the personal laws of Muslims, alleging genuine concern for Muslim women. But economic backwardness is a much more complex and bitterer reality for Muslim Indians. The state can't turn its eyes away, mainly when training many telescopes on the community's social issues.

It amounts to questioning the purity of the nationalism of Muslims, the same way the so-called upper castes have questioned the purity of the spiritualism of the so-called backward castes. Muslim Indians have neither compromised nationalism nor abandoned religion. India is depriving itself of one-fifth of its valuable talents by keeping Muslims backwards. The economic problems cannot be solved with civil rights remedies but could be relieved with public and private action encouraging economic redevelopment.

The economic agenda is more urgent for the community than most of the reforms the government is contemplating. The whole chorus of gender and other social reforms gives the impression that civil society faces multiple problems today. Most Muslims see these social reforms as a subterfuge for deflecting attention from the community's most pressing discrimination on the economic front.

The relative economic condition of Muslims has suffered significantly compared to everyone else despite spectacular growth in the country's economy. It makes for both good economics and politics if a fraction of new economic gain can correct the negative trajectory of the Muslim reality in India. Poor Muslims are much poorer than poor Hindus and can easily be bracketed with the lowest Hindu castes, Adivasis, and Dalits. Muslims are stuck at the bottom of almost every economic or social ladder.

All political parties at the helm of government have resorted to "strategic secularism" to secure the so-called Muslim vote bank. For this reason, Indian liberals have always couched Indian secularism in more progressive terms, namely, from a constitutional framework focused on supporting religious minorities to one that promotes community development, social justice, and cultural diversity.

Economic development cannot happen in a vacuum. It can be sustained only in a conducive social atmosphere. The comprehensive result is possible only when we have the rule of law, social harmony, equality before the law, respect for religion, and tolerance for diversity. In theory, politicians and preachers have always extolled a grand vision — that India historically has been a place of religious tolerance where settlers found a welcome melting pot in which everyone was free to practice their faith. This approach has stoked resentment among many of the country's Hindus while doing little to improve Muslims' well-being. This resentment will hit India's Muslims particularly hard, with further social and political marginalisation undermining their economic prospects. The size of India's Muslim population is bound to drag down overall development. In post-independent India, the state has paid lip service to this comforting tableau of the nation's pluralism.

Muslims Must Clear Their Minds about Shar'ia

Most of the world's nearly fifty Muslim-majority countries have laws referencing Shar'ia, the guidance Muslims believe God provided them on a range of spiritual and worldly matters. There is great diversity in how governments interpret and apply Shar'ia, and people often misunderstand its role in legal systems and the lives of individuals. However, there have been several myths that have distorted Islamic codes. Here is a list of the correct relationship between Shar'ia and the rules of Muslim society. Shar'ia is a religious code for Muslims that covers all aspects of their life, including daily routines, religious and familial obligations, marital affairs such as marriage and divorce, and financial dealings.

What is Shar'ia?

The word Shar'ia means "the path to a watering hole". It denotes an Islamic way of life that is more than a system of criminal justice. Shar'ia is a religious code for living in the same way the Bible offers Christians a moral system. The religious law of Islam is seen as the expression of God's command for Muslims and, in application, constitutes a system of duties that are incumbent upon all Muslims by their religious belief. Sharīʿah, the law, represents a divinely ordained path of conduct that guides Muslims toward a practical expression of religious conviction in this world and the goal of divine favour in the world to come. For believing Muslims, Shar'iah is the ideal realisation of divine justice — a higher law reflecting God's will.

Muslims have a wide range of beliefs about what Shar'iah requires in practice. All agree that humans are imperfect interpreters of God's will. But to ask a faithful Muslim if they "believe in" Shar'ia is to ask if they accept God's word. In effect, Shar'iah doesn't simply or exactly mean Islamic law. It is divine and unchanging, reflecting God's unity and perfection. It can be found in God's revealed word in the Quran and the divinely guided actions of the Prophet Muhammad. In contrast, Islamic laws are based on the level of competency in Shar'ia interpretations, not the length of study necessary to qualify as a jurist.

Shar'ia is derived from two primary sources: the Quran, considered the direct word of God, and hadith — thousands of sayings and practices attributed to the Prophet Mohammed that collectively form the Sunna. However, Shar'ia primarily comprises the interpretive tradition of Muslim scholars.

What Does Shar'ia Decree?

Shar'ia offers a code for living governing all elements of life, from prayers to fasting to donations to the poor. It decrees that men and women should dress modestly, which in some countries is interpreted as women wearing the veil and the sexes being segregated. Many states in the Middle East are incorporating more elements of Shar'ia into their state laws.

During the 19th century, the impact of Western civilisation on Muslim society brought about radical changes in civil and commercial transactions and criminal law. In these areas, the Shar'ia courts were perceived to be entirely out of touch with the needs of the time, not only because of their system of procedure and evidence but also due to the substance of the Shar'ia doctrine, which they were obligated to apply. As a result, Shar'ia's criminal and general civil law was abandoned in most Muslim countries and replaced by new codes based on European models. Thus, with the notable exception of the Arabian Peninsula, where Shar'iais still formally applied in its entirety, the application of Shar'ia law in Islam has been largely restricted, from the beginning of the 20th century, to family law, including the law of succession at death and the particular institution of waqf endowments. Islamic law varies by country, is influenced by local customs, and evolves. Shar'ia is also the foundation of legal opinions called fatwas, which Muslim scholars issue in response to requests from individual Muslims or governments seeking guidance on a specific issue. In Sunni Islam, fatwas are strictly advisory; in Shiite Islam, practitioners must follow the fatwas of their chosen religious leader.

Is Shar'ia an "Islamic Law?"

The most devout Muslims who conceptually embrace Shar'ia don't consider it a substitute for civil law. Shar'ia is not a book of statutes or judicial precedent imposed by a government, and it's not a set of regulations adjudicated in court. Instead, it is a body of Qur'an-based guidance that directs Muslims toward living an Islamic life. It doesn't come from the state, and it doesn't even come in one book or a single collection of rules.

Shar'ia is divine and philosophical. The human interpretation of Shar'ia is called "fiqh," or Islamic rules of right action, created by individual scholars based on the Qur'an and hadith (stories of the Prophet Muhammad's life). Fiqh means "understanding" — and its many different schools of thought illustrate that scholars knew they didn't speak for God.

The distinction between Shar'iah and fiqh matters especially because Muslims, including religiously traditional Muslims, do not agree with what Islamic law requires. They're disagreeing about what God wants, to be sure. But almost all faithful Muslims would say that they believe there is a single, truthful answer that lies in Shar'ia — we just cannot be certain as humans what that answer is.

How Religious Shar'ia Addresses Tolerance

Some critics argue that Muslim-led states that adhere to Shar'ia are particularly intolerant of non-believers or those who practice other religions. Scholars suggest that this intolerance largely arises from pre-modern restrictions imposed on non-Muslim minorities in Muslim lands, supported by certain Hadiths later incorporated into the Muslim canon that recommends the death penalty for Muslims who commit apostasy. Nigeria and Pakistan have implemented capital punishment for blasphemy and apostasy, as did Sudan for many years.

In addition, religious minorities in some Muslim countries have fewer rights under modern laws and are otherwise discriminated against. For instance, in Saudi Arabia, only Muslims are allowed to construct places of worship and pray in public. Some countries that claim to allow religious freedom, particularly authoritarian states, do not uphold this freedom in practice and routinely deny their citizens rights regardless of their faith.

What are Women's Rights in Shar'ia?

The Quran states that women are morally and spiritually equal to men but also indicates that wives and mothers have specific roles in the family and society. Particular Shar'ia guidance applies specifically to women, and some governments use Islamic law to significantly restrict women's rights, dictating how they dress and segregating them in specific spaces.

For example, Iran and Saudi Arabia have Islamic law-based regulations that require women to wear veils and be accompanied by male guardians in public places. Some Afghans and Western observers fear that Afghan women will face similar restrictions under the Taliban. Critics argue that these modesty rules create inequality by limiting women's education and employment opportunities. Other laws prevent women from initiating divorce and entering into marriage independently, contributing to child marriages and gender-based violence. Even in places where sexist laws have been abolished, attitudes and practices are slow to change or resistant to change.

Is There Room for Reforming Shar'ia?

Some Muslim scholars argue that the religious tenet of *Tajdid* allows practices under Shar'ia to be modified or eliminated. The concept is one of renewal, suggesting that Islamic societies should constantly reform to remain pure. At the same time, others consider that the purest form of Islam is the one practised in the seventh century.

Furthermore, there is significant debate over what the Qur'an sanctions versus what practices stem from local customs. For instance, Muslim feminists have long contended that sexist interpretations of Shar'ia originate from social norms, not Islam.

Modern governments have been known to amend laws considered to be Islamic. Saudi Arabia cited Islamic law when it granted women the right to drive in 2018. "It's yet another example that many rules called Islamic are often local, culturally influenced preferences that acquire an Islamic veneer."

In countries where Islam is the official religion, the Constitution designates Shar'ia as "a source," or sometimes "the source," of the law. Examples of the former include Afghanistan and Saudi Arabia, while Bahrain, Kuwait, and the United Arab Emirates are among those that apply Islamic law in personal but not civil or criminal matters. In Pakistan, Iran, and Iraq, it is forbidden to enact legislation antithetical to Islam. Non-Muslims are not expected to obey Shar'ia; in most countries, they are under the jurisdiction of special government committees and adjunct courts.

How Do Muslim Minority Countries Approach Shar'ia?

Some governments allow independent religious authorities to apply and adjudicate their faith's laws in certain situations. For instance, the United Kingdom (U.K.) permits Islamic tribunals governing marriage, divorce, and inheritance to make legally binding decisions if both parties agree. Additionally, Muslimminority countries such as Australia, Japan, the U.K., and the United States allow Islamic or Shar'ia-compliant banking.

Conversely, officials in certain Muslimminority countries seek to prevent Shar'ia from influencing state law or practice. Some have banned behaviours encouraged under Shar'ia, such as veil-wearing for women or ritual slaughter to make meat halal. The ban on wearing veils or headscarves exists in France, where secularism is part of the national identity, and conspicuous religious symbols are prohibited in specific public spaces.

Is Shar'ia Anti-woman?

Many Westerners perceive Muslim women's head coverings as a form of oppression. A verse in the Qur'an states that men are the "protectors" of women. Nonetheless, many contemporary scholars dispute the notion that this suggests women must obey men or that women are inferior.

While it's true that many majority-Muslim societies mistreat women, many of these laws, like Saudi Arabia's ban on female drivers, have no basis in fiqh. In instances where there is a fiqh origin for modern legislation, that legislation often cherry-picks specific rules, including more woman-affirming interpretations.

And on various issues, Islam can be fairly described as feminist. Fiqh scholars, for instance, have concluded that women have the right to orgasm during sex and to fight in combat. (Women fought alongside the Prophet Muhammad himself.) Fiqh can also be interpreted as pro-choice, with certain scholars positing that although abortion is forbidden, first-trimester abortions are not punishable.

Fiqh doctrine states that a woman's property, held exclusively in her name, cannot be appropriated by her husband, brother, or father. (For centuries, this contrasted sharply with women's property rights in Europe.) Muslim women in America are sometimes surprised to find that, even though they were careful to list their assets as separate, those assets can be considered joint assets after marriage. Fiqh has patriarchal rules, many of which are legislated in modern Muslim-majority countries.

Is Shar'ia About Conquest?

The Qur'an repeatedly commands Muslims to keep promises and uphold covenants. This includes treaties among nations and extends to individuals living under non-Muslim rule. Muslims have lived as minorities in non-Muslim societies since the beginning of Islam — from Christian Abyssinia to imperial China. Fiqh scholars have always insisted that Muslims in non-Muslim lands must obey the laws of those lands and do no harm within host countries. When local law conflicts with Muslims' Shar'ia obligations, some scholars suggest emigration, while others allow them to stay. None advocate violence or a takeover of those governments.

Where Shar'ia law is applied, it also varies. In Saudi Arabia, there are frequent executions and amputations, justified by selective readings of the Islamic holy texts. In other places, such punishments are rarely or never applied. In Saudi Arabia, too, women were not allowed to drive, but there has been some relaxation of this rule.

In Bangladesh and Pakistan, women can drive. Since there is no reference to motor vehicles in the Quran, the decision as to who can or can't drive them has been made by (male) Islamic scholars. Islamic states have repeatedly made efforts over centuries to co-opt and control the clergy, often with disastrous results.

The Future

Political Islamists recognise that further legal and administrative regulations must supplement the classical legal rules derived from the Quran and the Prophet Muhammad's actions. When they seek to incorporate Shar'iah into their constitutions, they usually request modern legislation informed by classical Islamic law and sometimes a rule that no legislation may violate classical Islamic legal regulations.

In Saudi Arabia, where no written Constitution exists, classical Islamic legal principles function as an unwritten, common-law Constitution. However, even Saudi Arabia has a body of administrative regulations that function similarly to legislation.

Muslims Need Redemption, Not Reforms

India has many things going for it these days, but the growing authoritarianism of Prime Minister Narendra Modi's right-wing Hindu nationalist government is not one of these. India's Muslims are the easy part of this story. The hard part is what has happened to our community. Every Indian Muslim knows about the pause: when another Indian, usually a Hindu, hears your name, waits a few seconds, and then, with a furrowed brow or a step back, acts surprised and confused that you, too, are Indian. The implication is suspicion, as though we are Indians with an asterisk—or worse, as though we are not Indians at all.

When they withdrew from the Indian subcontinent in 1947, paving the way for the independence of the newly partitioned nations of India and Pakistan, the Muslims of the region had a choice. They could resettle in Pakistan, where they would be among a Muslim majority, or remain in their original Indian homeland, where they would live as a minority in a majority-Hindu but constitutionally secular state.

India is a country of religious, ethnic, and linguistic diversity. Its estimated two hundred million Muslims, most of whom identify as Sunni, account for about 15 per cent of the population, by far the largest minority group. Hindus make up about 80 per cent of the people. The country's Muslim communities are diverse, with differences in language, caste, ethnicity, and access to political and economic power.

Economic Marginalisation of Minorities

When the country was partitioned, those who stayed back had traditionally been artisans, and most craft skills were overtaken by mechanisation, rendering most artisans' skills obsolete under the prevailing political economy. These people have lost their traditional livelihoods and cannot regain them in export markets, for instance, without government and business support. On the contrary, Hindu traders and business people have prospered from the country's booming economic growth.

The country's rulers must be prudent enough to realise that India's much-touted growth cannot be achieved if a vast section of its citizens feels unwelcome and targeted. When a community is repeatedly told that the forerunners of its faith were plunderers and were detrimental to the country, it is denied the deep historical ties of love and sacrifice that frame the identity of Muslim Indians and their place in the nation. The BJP can't hope to realistically make inroads among any section of the community if its policies end up pushing patriotic Muslims, who take great pride in their Indian identity, against the wall.

The government has taken a wide variety of policy initiatives for the development of minorities. Still, the general feeling among most of the Muslims is that these are cosmetic. Despite accelerated growth, the development deficit between them and others is increasing. There is a general perception among many Muslims that there seems to be some fear among various sections of society that the consequences of empowering Muslims by giving them unique benefits would strengthen communal politics in the country. This factor and the lack of necessary will on the parts of the Central and State Governments due to vote bank politics appear to have primarily dented the development process among minorities in the country.

The union government has passed several laws that have made life more difficult for religious minorities. This is aggravated by brash majoritarian rhetoric and the sectarian roots of the BJP, grounded in a perpetual and polarising social conflict between Hindus and Muslims. Several state governments have also passed anti-conversion laws that make converting people to a new religion illegal. The ostensible purpose of the measures is to stop proselytisation by Christians, which is their constitutional right, or to shield Hindus from Islam. But a conversion has historically promised members of the oppressed lower castes a way out of casteist society's repressive strictures. These are all attempts to scare minorities and make life miserable for them.

Demonisation of Minorities

Demonising minorities through bigoted policies and holding them responsible for all the national ills have become a favourite narrative. This script has repeatedly played itself out in history with disastrous consequences. Fundamentally, the state is trying to reconfigure the concept of Indian identity to make it synonymous with being Hindu. The right-wing attempts to dismantle India's secular traditions and turn the country into a religious state as a homeland for Hindus. The Muslims can see a shadow world creeping upon them. This dangerous game will pull apart the diverse, delicate social fabric that has existed in India for ages. India's founders advocated an Indian brand of secularism designed to hold the country's disparate communities together under one roof. Indeed, Jawaharlal Nehru pronounced India's composite culture as one of its greatest strengths.

Indian secularism is the by-product of a whole civilisation. According to the famous novelist and member of the Nehru family, Nayantara Sahgal, "We are unique in the world that so many cultures and religions enrich us. Now, they want to squash us into one culture. So it is a difficult time. We do not want to lose our richness. We do not want to lose anything. All that Islam has brought us, what Christianity has brought us, what Sikhism has brought us. Why should we lose all this? We are not all Hindus, but we are all Hindustani."

The Priority of the Economic Agenda

The economic agenda is more urgent for the community than most of the reforms the government contemplates because they involve a minuscule section of the population. The whole chorus of gender reforms gives an impression that the civil code is the prime urgency of the community and that it is a magic bullet for its multiple problems. But this is far from reality. Most Muslims see these gender reforms as a subterfuge for deflecting attention from the most pressing discriminations the community faces on the economic front.

Muslims have the lowest literacy rate and the highest percentage of illiterates aged beyond seven years (42.72 per cent), according to 2011 Census data. The number of illiterates is 36.4 per cent for Hindus, 32.49 per cent for Sikhs, 28.17 per cent for Buddhists, and 25.66 per cent for Christians, according to 2011 Census data on "education level by religious community" for age seven years and above.

In the literacy graph, Muslims are also the lowest among other religious communities. The Jain community has a 94.9 per cent literacy rate, Christians have 84.5 per cent, Sikhs 75.5 per cent, Hindus 73.3 per cent, and Muslims 68.5 per cent. The literacy rate among Muslims is lower than the national average of 74.04 per cent. The data also reveals that a meagre 2.76 per cent of Muslims are educated until graduation or above.

Despite almost trebling in the decade ending 2010 – from 5.2% to 13.8% – the rate of Muslim enrollment in higher education trailed the national figure of 23.6% and that of other backward classes (22.1%) and scheduled castes (18.5%). Scheduled tribes lagged Muslims by 0.5%. In proportion to their population, Muslims were worse off than scheduled castes and tribes. Muslims comprise 14% of India's population but account for 4.4% of students enrolled in higher education, according to the 2014-15 All-India Survey on Higher Education.

The Judicial View

The Supreme Court of India, through Chief Justice P.N. Bhagwati, expanded on the concept of the right to life not being a mere animal existence and declared in Francis Coralie's case [(1981) 1 SCC 608] that "the right to life is not a mere right to life under Article 21 and cannot be restricted to mere animal existence. It means much more than just physical survival, furthermore, the right to life includes the right to live with human dignity and all that goes along with it, namely, the bare necessities of life, such as adequate nutrition, clothing, shelter, and facilities for reading, writing, and expressing oneself in adverse forms, freely moving about, and mixing and mingling with fellow human beings..."

In the AkhilBharatiyaSoshitKaramchariSangh case (1981), Justice V R Krishna Iyer, while speaking for the court, explained that the right to equality without discrimination in public employment and reservation for backward classes under Article 16 of the Constitution were two sides of the same coin. Such interpretation was an insightful perception of our constitutional culture: "This is not mere harmonious statutory construction of Article 16(1) and (4) but an insightful perception of our constitutional culture, reflecting the current resurgent India bent on making, out of a sick and stratified society of inequality and poverty, a brave new Bharath. If freedom, justice, and equal opportunity to unfold one's personality belong alike to Bhangi and Brahmin, prince and pauper, if the panchama proletariat is to feel the social transformation, Article 16(4) promises, the state must apply equalising techniques that will enlarge their opportunities and thereby progressively diminish the need for props."

He added: "The authentic voice of our culture, voiced by all the great builders of modern India, stood for the abolition of the hardships of the pariah, the mlechchha, the bonded labourer, the hungry, hard-working half-slave, whose liberation was integral to our independence. To interpret the Constitution rightly, we must understand the people for whom it is made — the finer ethos, the frustrations, the aspirations, the parameters set by the Constitution for the principled solution of social disabilities."

Elucidating the argument, he said: "We, as judges dealing with a socially charged issue of constitutional law, must never forget that the Indian Constitution is a National Charter pregnant with social revolution, not a Legal Parchment barren of militant values to usher in a democratic, secular, socialist society that belongs equally to the masses, including the harijan-girijan millions hungering for a humane deal after feudal-colonial history's long night."

Welfare of Muslims

It is in this light that Muslims desperately need affirmative action in some form or rehabilitation through the infusion of credit through government programmes. Affirmative action refers to at least three measures available to help the socially disadvantaged: affirmative action, positive discrimination, strict school/college admissions, and job quotas. It can take many forms, from setting up special schools or vocational guidance facilities to declaring that the government will encourage specific groups to apply for jobs. Quota-based seats for castes and tribes in educational institutions, legislative bodies, and public offices were seen as a way of ensuring equal opportunity for people who had been excluded, subordinated, and denied social and economic resources. Caste-based distinctions, especially untouchability and forced segregation were seen as discrimination that placed the excluded community in a disadvantaged position. Reservations, above all, were an acknowledgement of this injustice and a means of bringing these hitherto ostracised sections into the social and political mainstream. The policy of reservations in government jobs for castes and tribes has, to some extent, guaranteed their participation in public employment.

Though the constitutionality of using religion as a criterion for selecting "backward" classes has not been explicitly challenged, the government and courts have rejected its application in practice; hence, minority groups were not identified as "backward" for special safeguards for the disadvantaged. There are three main reasons advanced: (i) it was incompatible with secularism; (ii) in the absence of a caste system among Muslims, there was no overt social discrimination suffered by them to justify special measures; and (iii) it would undermine national unity.

Affirmative Action

In India, reservations have been formulated on the principles of social justice enshrined in the Constitution. The Constitution provides for reservation for historically marginalised communities now known as backward castes. However, the Constitution does not define any of the categories identified for the benefit of reservation. One of the essential bases for reservation is interpreting the word "class".

Experts argue that social backwardness is a fluid and evolving category, with caste as just one of the markers of discrimination. Gender, culture, economic conditions, educational backwardness, and official policies, among other factors, can influence social conditions.

The notion of social backwardness could change as the political economy transforms from a caste-mediated closed system to a more open-ended, globally integrated, and market-determined system marked by high mobility and urbanisation. We are seeing this transformation at a much more exponential pace than our Constitution makers may have visualised.

In one of its well-known judgements, the Supreme Court has made an essential point about positive discrimination in India. Justices RanjanGogoi and Rohinton F. Nariman of the Supreme Court said, "An affirmative action policy that keeps in mind only historical injustice would certainly result in the protection of the most deserving backward class of citizens, which is constitutionally mandated. It is the identification of these new emerging groups that must engage the attention of the state."

We must actively consider evolving new benchmarks for assessing backwardness, reducing reliance on its caste-based definition. This alone can enable more contemporary groups to get the benefits of affirmative action through social reengineering, or else, the tool of affirmative action will breed new injustice. Muslims can become eligible for some forms of positive discrimination among new "backward" groups.

India has 3,743 backward castes and sub-castes, which comprise about half the population. So, the potential for caste warfare is endless. As British journalist Edward Luce wrote in his book "Despite the Gods," the result is "the most extensive system of patronage in the democratic world."

With such a rich gravy train, it's no wonder the competition turns lethal. The pervasive discrimination perpetrated on Indian Muslims must compel us to re-examine facile assumptions about social backwardness stemming from historically ignorant, simplistic, or outmoded categories. In a larger landscape of increasing communication, the government should economically and socially empower the community to develop appropriate solutions for overall social reforms.

Affirmative action has its limitations, as can be seen from its negative implications in India's social and political scenario. It has to be properly moderated, as its overdose can destroy the country's secular fabric. From being an instrument of egalitarianism, the reservation policy has resulted in blatant expression of what has come to be known as 'votebank politics'. This is particularly so regarding reservations for the OBCs in the post-Mandal scenario. It is here that affirmative action seems to have failed. Addressing one injustice or inequality at the cost of causing others can politicise society and damage its concepts of equality and egalitarianism. Both Parliament and the Court must critique reservation policies and legislation from a constitutional understanding of inclusive and integral justice.

A Policy of Harmonious Diversity

It is wise to remember the advice of Lyndon B. Johnson, "You do not examine legislation in the light of the benefits it will convey if properly administered, but in the light of the wrongs it would do and the harms it would cause if improperly administered."

It's absurd to try to consign the great diversity of our lives to one single identity, even one as splendid as the Indian tradition. Instead of constantly searching for a uniform and standardised culture, which would homogenise the entire population, we must strive for a stable and model democracy where the colours in the painter's palette find full expression. Therein lies the vibrancy of civilisation and the fulfilment of the pluralist promises of our Constitution.

Instead of using a binary of Muslims and non-Muslims, the state must adjust its lens and address the community's economic problems. Muslims have no more propensities for violence or anti-national sentiments than other Indians. Their faith encourages peaceful coexistence and mutual respect; liberal Muslims have given ample proof. This imbalance between Muslims and others must be recognised and addressed for India to retain its vitality as a plural society and vibrant civilisation.

The Future of Muslims in the Emerging India

The Indian prime minister was speaking from the historic Mughal era Red Fort in New Delhi, and the event marked the 400th birth anniversary celebrations of Guru Tegh Bahadur, the ninth Sikh guru. The occasion and the venue, in many ways, were appropriate. Modi reminded people of India's most despised Muslim ruler, who died over 300 years ago. "Back then, Aurangzeb severed many heads, but he could not shake our faith," Modi said during his address. His invocation of the 17th-century Mughal emperor was not a mere blip.

Aurangzeb Alamgir remained buried deep in the annals of India's complex history. The country's modern rulers are now resurrecting him as a brutal oppressor of Hindus and a rallying cry for Hindu nationalists who believe we must salvage India from the shame of the so-called Muslim invaders. The friction between Hindus and Muslims is a permanent feature of Indian life, and periodic bouts of bloody rioting are common. But since the rise of Prime Minister Narendra Modi and the BJP party, violence against Muslims has increased.

Hindu nationalist BJP encourages young Hindu men to become cow vigilantes who physically attack Muslims by brandishing their patriotism and faith. Even a rumour that a Muslim family ate beef for dinner or a Muslim man ferried a cow to a slaughterhouse can prove fatal in the hinterlands today.

They are attacked for marrying Hindu girls, sporting a beard, or wearing a skull cap or other symbols of religious identity. They are humiliated by popular, state-favoured news channels for being ungrateful betrayers and traitors who have no love for the national flag.

After 2019, we saw something new. We saw changes in the laws. A fundamental rule, for instance, was the Citizenship (Amendment) Act. It was passed to make religion the criterion for accessing Indian nationality. Only non-Muslim refugees from Bangladesh, Afghanistan, and Pakistan were eligible for citizenship. Also, the government passed new laws to make inter-religious marriages more difficult.

Revocation of Constitutional Article

There was also the revocation of Article 370, which had granted some autonomy to Kashmir, India's only Muslim-majority state. These laws were all passed simultaneously after the 2019 election. These elections transformed a de facto ethnic democracy into a de jure ethnic democracy. But they also marked a shift toward authoritarianism. And this authoritarianism took different forms.

First, we saw an attack on the judiciary. BJP tried to change the procedure for appointing judges. They failed. They forgot that Benjamin Netanyahu is on the precipice — not so much because of popular demonstrations but because the Supreme Court's judges said, no, we don't want to change how people are appointed. But, in retaliation, the Modi government refused to appoint the judges the judiciary had selected for the job. Therefore, in 2017, 2018, and 2019, you had a significant number of vacancies. And now, the court was on the defensive. They finally internalised this and stopped nominating judges they knew the government would not accept. They also started to become very complacent. So, either they validated any law the government passed or refused to take a stand.

The Citizenship (Amendment) Act is illegal, but the judges are sitting on it and don't want to give any verdict. The abolition of Article 370 was unlawful too. There are a significant number of laws that contradict the Constitution and which the judges should invalidate. That's one symptom of authoritarianism.

The press in India used to be vibrant, like the judiciary. That's over. The BJP used the leverage they had on the owners. The people who own the media in India are all businessmen. These businessmen have other businesses. They need the government's support, and if the government is not happy with some of the journalists, they ask the business people to ease out the journalists.

Modi seems more prevalent across India than it has much to do with the magnitude of anti-Muslim prejudice. It is so strong. People find refuge in the BJP against Muslims and Pakistan. It has a lot to do with the public sphere. They have propagated such diabolical images of Muslims that now it's deeply rooted in society's psyche. So, for that reason, you can say the popular support remains strong.

The scale of anti-Muslim prejudice in India and how it has openly infected many areas of Indian public life, especially in the past decade, is astonishing and depressing. I'm curious why you think that is or how it's happened.

You are against Muslims on the one hand, and you are against Hinduism on the other. These two factors are combined. But why has Hinduism become such an appealing identity? You can only understand it if you look at the modernisation of Indian society after 1991 when economic liberalisation resulted in more growth, urbanisation, and consumerism. These were the ingredients of a new middle class to become the core electorate of the BJP. This group became affluent but also rootless. They searched for an identity and found it in Hindu nationalism, which endowed them with cultural anchor points. This upper-caste middle class turned to new, modern, English-speaking gurus and sectarian movements in Gujarat and elsewhere. It started to follow the yoga classes of saffron-clad masters on television. The BJP has been very good at tapping that source of legitimacy by co-opting these gurus. More generally, the Ayodhya movement for building the temple in Ayodhya has enabled the BJP to capitalise on this appetite for Hinduism and pride in a Hindu identity.

Finally, they won because, in 2020, the Supreme Court of India said - go ahead, you can lay the first stone. Modi acts as though he were a priest as if he were the tremendous priestly head of India. You have a kind of theocracy in the making here, right? It explains an essential part of his popularity now that Modi is actively courting the world's gaze to felicitate his country's achievements.

Modi is keen to highlight the economic transformation he has presided over, making India an increasingly vital player on the world stage. And he is playing up his democratic bona fides.

But a much darker narrative is starting to define Modi's India. The government has been systematically oppressing, marginalising, and inciting hatred toward its 220-million Muslim minority. This campaign has been slowly gathering momentum over the years and has reached new intensity levels today. India is not a healthy democracy.

The toxic rhetoric is having an effect. Shortly after these speeches, during celebrations commemorating the birth of Lord Rama, multiple attacks took place all over the country. The most prominent attack saw about 1,000 Hindu rioters set fire to a century-old Muslim religious school in the northern state of Bihar. The rioters burned down the school library. The dangerous provocations continue.

Meanwhile, Modi was praising an extremely Islamophobic new film at a rally ahead of local elections this month.

Outside several civil society groups advocating for a pluralistic India and Muslim rights, the Supreme Court has been the most potent check on the BJP. However, even among the country's highest judges, there is a sense of exasperated helplessness. "The state is impotent. The state is powerless. It does not act in time. Why do we have a state if it remains silent?" Justice KM Joseph exclaimed during a recent hearing that condemned local BJP authorities for not prosecuting hate-speech violations at rallies.

What's happening in India is not that loose variety of internet fascism. It's the real thing. We have become Nazis. Our leaders, our TV channels, newspapers, and vast sections of our population have joined this brigade. Large numbers among the Indian Hindu population who live in the U.S., Europe, and South Africa support the fascists politically and materially. We must stand up for the sake of our souls and children's children. It doesn't matter whether we fail or succeed. That responsibility is not on us in India alone. Soon, if Modi wins in 2024, we will shut down all avenues of dissent. None of you in this hall must pretend to change the world with her writing. But it would be pitiful if she didn't even try.

Foreign nations that buy into the P.R. blitzkrieg calling India the world's largest democracy out of commercial and geostrategic interests or lazy naivety are complicit in the accelerating decline of democratic values in India. For now, the host of the G20 summit is reeling under one of the most undemocratic periods in its history. But now the time for warning is over. We are in a different phase of history.

Modi has tapped into a very deep-seated psychology among members of the diaspora who want to recover lost pride in the rise of a great civilisation that has been wronged through colonisation. No one ever bothered about the so-called Hindu identity before. People have transitioned from being normal, ordinary people into Hindu fundamentalists. India has come onto the world stage. Divisions within the Indian diaspora have expressed themselves in other ways. Descendants of the historically oppressed Dalit community have led a push to ban caste discrimination, pitting them against upper-caste Hindus. Today, the balance between Canada and India has shifted. Thirty years ago, the Indian economy needed Canada. Now it's a 180-degree opposite. Canada needs India. India is the growing economic and military power, not Canada.

The Shattered Muslim Hope in India

More than seven decades have passed since the struggle of the Indian subcontinent to free itself from British imperial rule was crowned with success. For half a century or more before emancipation, nationalists of both the tremendous religious communities were confident that communal antipathy was illusory - a mere creation of the British Raj, based on the traditional particularly Roman maxim, of "divide and rule." Our post-independence history has shown that antagonism between Muslims and Hindus is much more deeply rooted than in factors that cannot be so easily simplified. The ink was not yet dry on the 1947 Charter of Sovereignty before one great single nation under British rule split into two hostile countries, Pakistan and India, and the hopes of harmony between two cultural allies were belied.

The chaos, confusion, and religious violence that followed the separation of Pakistan from India 75 years ago resulted in the deaths of up to two million people and unleashed one of history's largest displacements, with Hindus and Muslims from once-mixed communities rushing in opposite directions to new homelands in such great haste that it appeared an act of insanity.

In the decades since the divisions have become extremely rigid and violent. To this day, despite a vast shared heritage, the two countries remain estranged, their guns fixed on each other, and diplomatic ties all but nonexistent. In both, majoritarian populism is ascendant. India is gripped by rising Hindu nationalism and anti-Muslim sentiment, with the ruling party trampling constitutionally mandated secularism. Pakistan is swept by Islamic fundamentalism that has made life miserable for both the rulers and citizens. The population of Kashmir, the Himalayan region disputed between the two countries, remains hostage to militarism and militancy from each side.

A Shared Inheritance

A vast generation of succeeding troupes and guilds of artists from both the Hindu and Muslim communities conceived and produced resourceful creativity that propelled pre-modern South Asians to build a syncretic, convivial, and broadly pluralistic society. Meanwhile, in India, founded at the same time on a promise of secular democracy, a Hindu supremacist regime wants to purify the country's so-called impure past, expunging all traces of "Muslim influences," including the Taj Mahal.

In many ways, the binary constructs of "Indian" and "Pakistani" are a reminder of how hastily British-ruled India was split in two: the Partition entailed massacres, large-scale displacement, and unhealable bitterness. The struggles for personal power between leaders of the new nations were locked in right from their birth, and today history books are being purged of Muslim heritage.

The political history of their 75 years has been marred by bitterness, cold wars, minority pogroms, and minimal protections for the poor and weak – provokes mostly despair and foreboding. Hopes for a survivable present and viable future depend a great deal on how we understand our rich history. Violence and brutality were hardly unknown to it, and places of worship were never desecrated. There are millennia-old traditions, values, and compassion that continue to exemplify peace and coexistence in many spaces.

The BJP has always considered Muslims to be less Indian than Hindus. The political party was formed in 1980 as an offshoot of the RashtriyaSwayamsevakSangh (RSS), an all-male paramilitary organisation founded in 1925. Throughout Modi's premiership, which began in 2014, he has turned India into an increasingly illiberal democracy. Vigilante attacks on religious minorities have increased markedly.

Marginalisation of Muslims

The South Asian nation's most significant minority forms some 14 per cent of the country's 1.3 billion population, but only four per cent are represented in the Lok Sabha. It is the lowest Muslim representation in five decades, compared with more than six per cent a decade ago and a peak of 9.6 per cent in 1980. Many young Muslims express pessimism about the future of Muslim politics in the country currently ruled by Prime Minister Narendra Modi's ruling Hindu nationalist Bharatiya Janata Party (BJP).

Representation or giving seats in an election is primarily winnability-driven. We have had Muslim candidates also, and [if] more such winnable candidates are part of the party fold, they indeed will find their opportunities. However, the most significant challenge is the poor solidarity among Muslim voters, which has resulted in the self-destruction of several winnable and competent Muslim contenders for this seat. The Hindu consolidation has largely been achieved with remarkable success and consolidations, by vilifying Muslims and spreading hatred against them.

BJP wants a uniform world, as opposed to one guided by pluralism. BJP's electoral majority has made it "indifferent to minority politics. In recent decades, most secular parties and the Indian National Congress, which prides itself on having fought for India's independence with the ideals of plurality and secularism, have all started to shun Muslims. With the formidable rise of the BJP, other political parties have also become hesitant in fielding many Muslim candidates. The Congress, particularly the BJP's main rival, has reduced the number of tickets to Muslims due to fear that it would backfire electorally. Even other political parties, with their claims of secularism, have failed to take on the BJP on its anti-Muslim stance. No one is willing to confront the BJP on its practice of excluding Muslims. They are doing it not out of fear of being branded pro-Muslim but because they are apprehensive that they will lose the sympathy of Hindus.

The Vote Bank Politics

While India's Muslims have held high-profile constitutional posts, including the President and Chief Justice, despite all this positivity, the community remained under-represented in democratic and government institutions. In 1947, most Muslims did not migrate to Pakistan when British India partitioned the country into Muslim-majority Pakistan and Hindu-majority India. In India's first national elections in 1952, only 11 Muslims could enter parliament. As political parties wouldn't allocate too many seats to Muslims due to an evident lack of legitimacy of Muslim candidates and a climate of suspicion against Muslim politicians, Muslims require quality leaders who can intervene inside and outside the legislative arena.

The Congress mopped up Muslim votes, which did not translate into political representation. That practice lies at the root of skewed secularism. The Congress looked at Muslims only as a "vote bank" and did little to promote leadership within the community. When Britain partitioned India, tens of millions of Muslims chose a secular India as their homeland; they were betting on a more promising future in a country that enshrined religious equality in its Constitution. But Hindu nationalists have long claimed a more significant moral right over the nation and have questioned the patriotism of Indian

Muslims. And the prejudice is no longer just rhetorical. It has turned into violent hatred spilling onto the country's streets.

The shift in India's attitude toward minorities is being met with resistance and response by writers, artists, and activists. Muslims have consciously chosen to place their destiny in the hands of a secular India, believing in the guiding principles of democracy. That faith is now put to the test every day. In Modi's India today, as acts of communal violence increase, the worst fears of Indian Muslims are coming true.

What Muslims need to counter their fears is solidarity among themselves and nurturing quality leaders whom they recognise and acknowledge wholeheartedly. This can help their representation in all the important spheres and give them bargaining strength at the negotiating table. The tragedy is that most Muslim votes are being funnelled by political parties to defeat their possible opponents. Most Muslim votes are being wasted, resulting in a great loss to the community's united strength.

The Indian judiciary, the supposed sentinel of my rights and freedoms, has been the biggest let-down among all the country's institutions. The pen of the judge moves with great alacrity to sign the bail orders of those who have shot at Muslims, bombed them, and called for genocide against them, but so rarely to protect Muslims from the state's or the majority's harm or to dispense justice for the atrocities committed against them. And the words spun by the lordships — way of life, the preponderance of probabilities, collective conscience — have gone on to become the mainstay of the tall structures that perpetuate injustice and oppression.

Justice is a basic human need; the lack of it can be so deeply unsettling. The Lordships need to realise that it can't be offered in crumbs here and there; it needs to be absolute and abundant. I, for one, am not big on speedy justice. It can take its own sweet time to arrive, but when it does, it should make the heart full. And that is what makes you love a place; you can never truly love a place that doesn't give you justice. With that realisation, came the explanation as to why I had felt so conflicted all these years.

The Tinctured Canvas of India's Rich Diversity

The Partition of India, which led to the deaths and displacement of millions of people and the creation of two countries, occurred more than years ago. The 15th of August 1947 was seared into the collective consciousness of Indian and Pakistani people across the world, as India was freed from the British Empire and split into two. In the end, Radcliffe and his team—none of whom had any understanding of Indian history, society, and culture—split both provinces in two and awarded roughly half to each new nation. This meant the new country of Pakistan would not be a contiguous nation: Most of its landmass lay in the Northwestern corner of India, with a chunk called East Pakistan that lay in Bengal in the West. What became the 'Radcliffe Line' – the border that divided the country into two entities, split communities, and divided families, and the British authorities' decision to grant sovereignty has been criticised for its haste. The Partition gave birth to a terrible refugee crisis, with some 15 million displaced people forced to leave their homes to travel to Pakistan, India, and elsewhere.

Writing for *The Guardian*, historian and Oxford lecturer Dr Yasmin Khan blames the British for the inopportune timing of the Partition and subsequent violence: "The British government had repeatedly delayed granting freedom in the 1930s when it might have been more amicably achieved... the planning was shoddy, and the date was rushed forward by a whole year; the original plan was for a British departure in mid-1948. The British come out of the story looking ill-prepared, naive, and even callous."

After gaining independence from Britain in 1947, India did two crucial things. It gave all citizens the right to vote, and it adopted a secular Constitution that enshrined equality before the law. But during the last decade, some of that high-mindedness and nobility of social, cultural, and political ethos have eroded. Corruption and "goondah-raj" (thug rule) politics have tarnished Indian democracy. The enduring reality of caste and class privilege has undermined the ideal of equality. Modi's abrasive rule against Muslims and his ambition of turning democracy into a Hindutva model has eroded India's original culture of diversity.

Large sections of Hindus, Muslims, and Sikhs challenged the greatest imperialist power, Britain, during India's first war of independence on May 10, 1857. This extraordinary unity, naturally, unnerved the Britons and made them realise that if their rule was to continue in India, it could happen only when Hindus and Muslims, the two largest religious communities, were divided along communal lines. Urgent steps were taken to create enmity between these two groups. This was why, immediately after crushing this liberation war militarily, the then Minister of Indian Affairs, Lord Wood, sitting in London, confessed: "We have maintained our power in India by playing off one part against the other, and we must continue to do so. Do all we can, therefore, to prevent all having a common feeling."

It is a reenactment of the same British in crushing Muslims. India has been held together for seven decades by its Constitution, which promises equality to all. But Narendra Modi's BJP is remaking the nation into one where some people count as more Indian than others. Prime Minister Modi is inflaming hatred of Muslims in India as the world looks the other way. Hindu hardliners, one holding a sword, chant slogans against Muslim communities. A darker narrative is starting to define Modi's India. The government has been systematically oppressing, marginalising, and inciting hatred toward its 220-million Muslim minority. This campaign has been slowly gathering momentum over the years and has reached new intensity levels today. India is not a healthy democracy.

The Trajectory of Hindutva

The controversy that has convulsed into a violent India has roots in the era of the British Raj. Whereas the mainstream of India's independence movement envisioned a secular, inclusive republic, Hindu nationalists saw religion as the strongest base for a new national identity. They resented the creation of Pakistan, the new state demanded by Muslim separatists, yet in effect wanted India to be a Hindu version of such a religion-based nation. It was the secular vision which prevailed, and which remained unchallenged and fully protected until the 1980s. But in the 1990s, a mixture of fatigue with the long rule of the Congress party, plus a wave of local sectarian disputes caused in part by the emergence of jihadism as a global menace, began to consolidate more Hindus behind the HindunationalistBharatiya Janata Party (BJP). This was the impetus that gave rise to the erosion of liberalism and secularism. The end of secularism was very much in sight, and its slide was much faster than what could have been anticipated. Several political parties found it expedient to denounce Muslims to gain Hindu sympathy for burnishing their political credentials. The Modi government's rhetoric and policies often favour the Hindu majority, and Modi's tenure has been marked by "controversy and criticism as well as resounding electoral success. Founded 94 years ago by men besotted with Mussolini's fascists, the RSS (the original organisation from which emerged the BJP) is the holding company of Hindu supremacism: of Hindutva, as it's called. Given its role and size, finding an analogue for the RSS anywhere in the world is complicated. In nearly every faith, the source of conservative theology is its hierarchical, centrally organised clergy; that theology is recast into a project of religious statecraft elsewhere by other parties. Hinduism, though, has no principal church, no single pontiff, and nobody to ordain or rule. The RSS has appointed itself as the arbiter of theological meaning and the architect of a Hindu nation-state. It has at least 4 million volunteers, who swear oaths of allegiance and participate in quasi-military drills.

Since the ruling Hindu nationalist Bharatiya Janata Party (BJP) came to power, incidents of sectarian violence targeting the Muslim minority, who make up about 14% of the population, have become increasingly frequent. Hardline vigilante Hindu right-wing groups have been emboldened under the Modi regime, and there is nothing to restrain them from carrying out sustained persecution and lynchings of Muslims in BJP-controlled territories. Muslims have been described as "intruders," faced discriminatory policies, and had their homes bulldozed. Yet, as India heads towards an election next year with Modi expected to win a third term, many fear such flare-ups of violence will continue to worsen as the pursuit of electoral victories splinters society further down religious lines. Modi has so far remained silent on this week's events.

Muslims in India

Muslim Indians have neither compromised nationalism nor abandoned religion. India is depriving itself of one-fifth of its valuable talents by keeping Muslims backwards. The economic problems cannot be solved with civil rights remedies but could be relieved with public and private action encouraging economic redevelopment. Friction between Hindus and Muslims is a permanent feature of Indian life, and periodic bouts of bloody rioting are common. In what appears to be a pattern of targeting Muslims, India has also passed a new citizenship law that could open the door to legal discrimination against Muslims. At the same time, law enforcement agencies have looked the other way on bloody violence directed against Muslims. There's little doubt that Modi's rule has emboldened the proponents of Hindutva, who believe India should be a Hindu nation. It is a big challenge for Indian Muslims to deal with powerful sections of the Hindu majority, bent on mixing religion with politics and entrenching communalism.

It's important to remember that Muslims are India's most significant minority, over 14 per cent of the population. There was a time when Hindus and Muslims jointly fought for freedom against British colonial rule. They firmly rejected the theory, propagated by power-hungry politicians, that Hindus and Muslims cannot live together in one country. Today, to suggest that Indian Muslims are anti-national and aliens, as some do, is preposterous.

Despite political and social exclusion threats, Muslims haven't retreated into a shell or adopted violent means of resistance. Indian Muslims have the advantage that, unlike other authoritarian Asian states, India is a democracy. It has a secular Constitution which may have been diluted by the new agenda, a vibrant democracy, an independent judiciary, an impartial electoral process, and an army that stays away from politics. The press can no longer be counted on to play an honest role. It is time for Muslims to test India's institutions for legal redress and constitutional protection.

The fact is that Indian Muslims, like all Indians, are concerned about poverty, employment, and education. A slowing economy and increased joblessness hurt everyone. The Indian economy is expected to grow at its lowest rate in over a decade. Social disharmony, economic slowdown, and rising poverty threaten India's progress. They hurt Modi's image as a robust and business-oriented leader. If the economy continues its downward slide, Modi may need to use all his charm to control a mob of disaffected followers. It would be preposterous for him to assume that the protests and violence will die out, and it will be business as usual. The writing on the wall is clear, and it is for him to act fast to reverse India's growing violence, unemployment, and poverty.

Secularism in Modi's India

The situation has gone beyond dismissing the opposition as "anti-national" and "termites" determined to derail India's rise to the world stage. The government focuses less on urgent economic issues and more on its narrow social and political agenda. India is losing leverage and strong clout in South Asia as its government tries to recast the country into a Hindu state, stripping it of its secular and liberal values. In marginalising and victimising its minority Muslims at home, the BJP government has weakened India's traditional and acclaimed policies of encouraging harmony as a leader demonstrating these values in its important role in this region. The changed policies have led to many fault lines that have certainly become irreparable. It is difficult to fathom whether we can retrieve our respected role, which had been built with great efforts by leveraging several positive virtues of the nation. The shift could also open opportunities for China, which has used the promise of investment and access to its hard-charging economy to cultivate stronger relations with its rival neighbours. It is no longer just our leaders we must fear, but a whole section of the population. The banality of evil and the normalisation of corruption are now manifest in our streets, classrooms, and many public spaces. The mainstream press and the hundreds of 24-hour news channels have drafted to the cause of fascist majoritarianism. The government subtly reoriented India's Constitution to suit its ideology. Modi's government has adopted laws and policies discriminating against religious minorities, and his supporters have carried out killings and acts of violence against them, often with impunity. But criticism from Western nations seeking closer economic ties with India and a geopolitical counterweight to China has been muted.

It must be time for some introspection and course correction. Modi and the BJP can reassure the country that they have no intention to suppress dissent and subvert national institutions to gain political mileage. At the same time, they should assure minorities, particularly Indian Muslims, that they are an integral part of Indian society and that the government firmly opposes violence and discrimination against their vulnerable population. Social harmony is important in India's triumphant global march to its rightful place, which it has already achieved in several spheres on the world stage.

India's Role

India must not forget that it has a heavy moral responsibility cast upon it. India, in its seventy-fifth year, has stood tall in the comity of nations as a plural, secular democracy. For centuries, it has evoked boundless rare opportunity to be the epicentre of innumerable faith traditions along with unprecedented contact with the world's many cultures. Few countries can boast of such unity in diversity. India can still retain its oral glory, and it is time it realises that it will be paying a heavy price by abandoning the values and virtues that have given it this glorious stature.

For India, championing the idea of religious harmony is not a narrow necessity of electoral politics. Its nationalism is not based on language, geography, ethnicity, or religion but on a land emerging from an ancient civilisation united by a shared history and sustained by a pluralist democracy.

'VasudhaivaKutumbakam' (the whole world is one family)," a Sanskrit phrase found in the texts of the Maha Upanishad, is a key concept embodying peaceful coexistence, diversity, and secularism within

its structure, is engraved in the entrance hall of the Parliament of India.

The sentiment of religious harmony, likewise originating in the ancient Indian scripture of the Rigveda, admirably displays the plurality of religious thought with its mention of "*Ekam Sat VipraBahudhaVadanti*" (wise people explain the same truth in different manners). It also literally means, "Truth is one, the wise perceive it differently."

India's call for unity and solidarity, regardless of religion, language, or ethnicity, is the idea of one nation that excludes none and accepts differences. In his historic speech in the Parliament of World Religions, Chicago, in 1893, Swami Vivekananda said, "If the Parliament of Religions has shown anything to the world, it is this: It has proved to the world that holiness, purity, and charity are not the exclusive possessions of any church in the world and that every system has produced men and women of the most exalted character."

The Past and Present of Islam

Islam is today the religion of more than 1.7 billion followers, with Muslims inhabiting a wide belt stretching from the Atlantic to the Pacific, encompassing Africa, parts of Europe, and Asia. Muslims exhibit a similar interest in studying the reality of Islam, to understand to what extent they can adopt modern ways without compromising their religion.

Modern Muslim thinkers discover in the principles of Islam a flexibility that permits them to explain and interpret with the greatest freedom while still preserving their faith.

In this process of expansion, Islam interacted with foreign religions and cultures, influencing and being influenced. If the chief locus of influence was literary and linguistic, there was an exchange at the most profound levels of theology. As Rome moved toward a position of mediation between God and man, Islam, more in the spirit of the Christian Reformation, preserved the teaching in the Koran of Allah's closeness to man. The Koran says: "Unto Allah belong the East and the West, and whithersoever ye turn, there is Allah's countenance" (2/115), and, "And We are nearer to him (man) than his jugular vein " (50/16). There is no priest in the Muslim's mosque praying for him; he directs his prayer directly to the Deity. There is no doubt that the world needed this doctrine, just as it needed the Christian doctrine that came before it. It received these two doctrines at their destined times.

Islam was much affected by the cultures over which it spread. New religious and philosophical schools were set up due to the interaction between Islam and Greek philosophy; it also absorbed certain Indian and Persian mystical tendencies. The Mutazilites subjected the texts of religion to Greek rationalism, while the Sufis brought in an element of mysticism and ecstasy, which Islam lacked. Dervish preaching on the necessity of mediation between God and His slave, man, led in some periods and regions to a sort of cult of saints. The stimulation of these various tendencies produced a series of brilliant philosophers who were studied with respect in medieval Europe.

The rapid spread of Islam over a huge area broke down a number of the social ideals of the early Muslim community. The spirit of Islam—Mohammed's reform of the society he had found—allowed a certain laxity to develop later: multiple marriages became a problem and easy divorce an evil, while the social equality of early Islam gave way to the customs of the conquered despotic empires.

It is against the backdrop of a long and wearisome "Dark Age" that modern Islam must be viewed. It must be remembered that at least 70% of the Arabs today are illiterate and that, at the same time, the new stimulus to change in Islamic society is, unlike the outside stimuli in earlier eras, almost entirely secular. Traditional Islam was a complete "way of life" in which social conventions and religious beliefs were closely integrated. Today, Islam is moving toward a position more like that of Western religion, with separation of church and state. This is reflected in education.

There is no school in Muslim countries in which religious studies do not exist. But the teacher of religion is usually not also a teacher of secular studies. The two fields are becoming entirely independent of each other. Thus, Egypt, for example, has alongside and separate from its ancient Azhar—the world's oldest university—three modern, secular universities, which are largely Western in organisation and spirit.

The central problem facing Arab Muslims, and indeed all Muslims, today is how to find a new way of life—Islamic in character—which will be halfway between the East and the West and which will provide the internal stability necessary to enable Muslims to face their problems independently. The Arab World can borrow technology from the West, but it must find the answers to its deeper problems within itself. One only needs to observe book-buying habits to see that the strong interest in Islam is still alive today. In Cairo, any book discussing Islam is sure to be a big sale. This shows that people are not drifting away from religion. It is a fact that the world struggle between democracy and communism has led Muslims to make a fresh evaluation of their religion to see where it stands regarding these two conflicting movements.

How far does Islam penetrate the hearts of Muslims today? What tangible effects does it have in their lives? There is no simple answer, and much depends on exactly what is meant by Muslims. Those who have a good understanding of Islam—unfortunately, the minority—are inspired by their religion with pride, self-respect, and a desire for freedom. The Muslim Brotherhood is the extreme expression of this side of Islam. Hasan el-Banna, the founder of the movement, called on Muslims to be "leaders in their countries and masters in their homelands." There is no wonder that the past glory of Islam arouses feelings of pride and desire for freedom. This spirit underlay this century's continuous revolts against foreign rule, and we see it at work now in North Africa.

Islam inspires its followers to sanctify the mind, reject the miraculous, and meditate on God's creation to confirm belief. Mohammed did not prove the validity of his message by miracles. The Koran is full of verses which call us to the knowledge of God through reason alone. Abdu maintained that Islam demands faith in God and His unity through rational inference and that the belief in God should come before the belief in the prophecies. "It is not proper that the belief in God should be taken from the words of the prophets nor the revealed Book, because it is unreasonable to believe in a Book revealed by God unless one already believes in the existence of God."

Islam instructs its followers to believe in this world and the world to come in such a way as not to have one overpower the other. The Muslim has the right to enjoy the pleasures of this world because it was created for him. "But seek the abode of the Hereafter in that which Allah hath given thee and neglect not thy portion of the world, and be thou kind even as Allah hath been kind to thee, and seek not corruption in the earth; lo! Allah loveth not corruptors" (28/77). There is a well-known proverb widely spread among Muslims: "Work for this world as though you will live forever, and work for the next world as though you will die tomorrow."

Different Muslims have reacted to the incursion of Western ideas diversely. The Egyptian writer Ahmad Ameen said frankly: "The reform of Islam will come about in two ways: one, by separating science from religion, and advancing in science as extensively as possible; the other, through the practice of absolute *Ijtihad*." *Ijtihad* means "free interpretation," and Ahmad Ameen goes on to explain: "We do not mean by this the use of the mind only and the blind imitation of the foreigner, but we mean that kind of *ijtihad* achieved by those who are qualified, a kind that would understand its aims, and also understand Western civilisation and its aims; then allow or prohibit in the light of these two kinds of understanding."

Another contemporary Muslim writer has advocated implicitly that free interpretation should be applied to matters about Islamic doctrine and not to matters of jurisprudence alone. But the conditions of Muslims today do not yet permit this absolute freedom of interpretation, though they are moving toward it.

A third position, which calls for the separation of religion from the state, but not from society, has been advocated by Sheikh Ali Abdel-Razik in his book *Islam and Principles of Rule* and by a powerful writer of the younger generation, Khalid Mohammed Khalid, whose *From Here We Start* has been widely read. While to be sure, the Muslim Brotherhood disagrees with this line of thought, the majority of cultured Muslims tend to endorse it. Almost all of the Muslim world now uses secular civic law, with some slight Islamic modifications rather than the old religious code. Only the laws covering "personal status"—marriage, divorce, inheritance, and the like—have remained unchanged. Even the old Muslim code is civil to some extent, particularly in marriage, which is carried out by a written contract, the conditions of which are dictated by both parties. There are also certain traditional concepts which facilitate the modification of Muslim law; the idea of "free interpretation" applies in this field, as does that of "consensus." Thus, if enough Muslims unanimously agree upon a certain matter, it becomes a religious law. The Muslim Brotherhood›s call to return to religious legislation is one of its programme's weakest points and has caused continuous disputes with the various Egyptian governments to this day.

The jurist el-Banna expressed the liberal view when he wrote: "We should know that the glorious Koran is not based upon the laws... It contains six thousand verses, and the total number of verses concerned with laws does not exceed five hundred.

The Koran is concerned rather with the training of character and the cleansing and purification of the spirit." This means that legislation should be considered a means and not an end. Ahmad Ameen went even further, claiming that only fifty verses of the Koran and 17 Traditions of the Prophet were concerned with law. He called for absolute free interpretation on condition that the spirit of Islam be truly understood. And not long ago, the Egyptian Minister of Waqf (Muslim Endowments), who is a learned man of the Azhar, approved of Muslims paying and receiving interest on charitable trust investments—a "modern point of view which is nevertheless in keeping with the spirit of Muslim legislation.

The time has come, I believe, for Christians and Muslims to understand that they are in the same boat: if it sinks, they will all sink; if it remains afloat, they will all be saved. There must be sincere cooperation in both the spiritual and material life. And this will only be accomplished with a sound basis of mutual respect, confidence, and tolerance.

What It's Like to Be a Muslim in Today's India?

Do not show the face of Islam to others; instead show your face as the follower of true Islam representing character, knowledge, tolerance and piety

– Sir Syed Ahmed Khan
(17 October 1817 – 27 March 1898)

An educated, secular and liberal Indian Muslim is in a bind; he is torn between finding the right balance between loyalty to his faith and adherence to the new tests of patriotism being imposed by certain intolerant groups. The high-voltage saffronisation wave that is demonising Muslims has broken the resistance of even strong neutral and secular groups who are now inclined to go with the official tide. The centuries-old secular souls are slowly being ruptured. India has suddenly become deaf to its minorities, who are shuddering with muteness at the growing intolerance of saffron hordes. Mocking and ridiculing of Muslims is now rife in public spaces.

India's once cherished and internationally lauded secular values have been drowned in the sea of primitive majoritarian politics, which is driven more by uncontrollable rage than by sensible reason. Not just Hindutva foot soldiers but democratic institutions and spaces are being used to suppress religious freedom. We are fast seeing a potential breakdown of what was a flourishing multicultural society. Muslims are made to routinely confront a culture of fear which sees everything Muslim as pure evil.

I can feel the disdain emanating from officers when they look at my passport and find I have a Muslim name. Other friends — much richer and better known than most of us — will tell you how difficult it is to rent a house if you are a Muslim. A sense of despair runs through the entire Muslim community, and they are passing through the most horrific phase post-Partition.

Continuing inebriation on account of political popularity has emboldened the intolerant elements in the ruling party, who are now openly imposing their moral benchmarks about diet, dress, faith and patriotism, overlooking the cultural sentiments of others. This rhetoric is injecting anti-Muslim sentiments into a climate where Muslims are already feeling alienated and marginalised. The political and social environment has never been so hostile. An ordinary Muslim is being hissed and snarled with vileness by all and sundry in full glare of the law.

Several questions keep agitating a Muslim's mind. I am a patriotic and secular Indian, and then

- Why do people stare at me when I wear my skull cap or Hijab?
- Why does my name force people to doubt my love for my nation?
- Why do I hear comments like "You will be supporting Pakistan during a match"?
- Why do I not get a good apartment on rent in a posh locality?
- Why do people call me staunch if I pray five times a day?
- Why am I called an orthodox Muslim if I follow my religion to the best of my capacities?
- Why are the boys of my community under constant surveillance?
- Why am I not an Indian as much as you are?

The majority of Indian Muslims not only have to worry about worsening communal relations and police brutality but also face high unemployment and widespread poverty. They live in urban ghettos or squalid villages and suffer from ignorance, ridicule, humiliation, and The profound sense of pain caused by calculated and senseless ridicule of their religious practices only serves to alienate them from the national mainstream.

India must not forget that it has an entire generation of young Muslims who were born into a turbulent era and whose mindset and identity are being nurtured in an environment where they apprehend being suspected as 'disloyal others'. Some of them are highly talented and are in the vanguard of the nation's new development revolution.

The negative profiling of Muslims can cause alienation among the Muslim community, and as a result of this alienation, there will be enough space for fissiparous tendencies, leading to long-term fissures. Studies have shown that one of the factors underpinning radicalisation is a sense of loss of belonging and identity.

Muslims have been forced to think deeply about their role in the present-day political climate in India. It isn't so much a battle of what it means to be a Muslim in India. It's a greater battle between broader India of how tolerant and open-minded it will be about minorities, about Indian values of democracy and secularism, about recognising how true they want to be to the Indian values of openness and freedom for all.

Of late, the Indian secular fabric is increasingly becoming fragile. Many on either side don't believe in either tolerance or moderation and are determined to follow the age-old adage 'paying them in their coin' too literally. The official machinery, which had earlier been by and large very subtle in its communal agenda, is now baring its fangs brazenly.

Religion is often portrayed simply as a social or political construct, although for millions of people, religion is a daily practice and the very real framework of an understanding that connects human lives to a spiritual reality. For the laity, faith is the prism through which they view the world, and their religious communities are their central environments. For them, it is a benign force, shorn of the political sentiments which are manipulated into an ideological construct by ideological groups for their election algorithms.

It is difficult to overstate the importance of faith in the lives of people for whom it is a creed of peace and love. Most people would prefer to live in peace than in conflict. At their very core, all religions espouse peace, tolerance and compassion. Yet, often, the only religious voices on the front pages are those speaking messages of hatred or violence, especially in stories about conflict or social tensions. One of the best ways of breaking down barriers between faiths is by building relationships and getting to know each other. It's not just a platitude but it is a verse from the Q'uran where the Lord says, 'He made us different so we can get to know each other.'

Taking that verse to heart, getting to know other people, and coming together on issues that are common to all of us can synergise a new spirit of bonhomie. We're all concerned with education and poverty, growing inflation, surging unemployment and taxes, where we can find common ground and work towards a better world and better future for all of us.

There is much in common among people, irrespective of the faith they profess. It is this which needs to be explored. We need to be able to see the other and say, 'We understand you are different, but we also understand the difference'.

There is ample scope for reconciliation if only we are willing to avail ourselves of the myriad opportunities staring at us. Despite the many superficial differences, all our deeper and more permanent values are similar. The respect for knowledge, justice, truth, compassion towards the less privileged, commitment to healthy family life, and the striving to improve our world and make it a better place for everyone are commonalities to people of all faiths. A more sobering reflection can help us smoothen the ridges that keep straining our relationships.

The majority must realise that minorities face a severe emotional complex. An ordinary Muslim carries a lot of weight on his shoulders, having a lot of responsibility. Having a responsibility to his community and responsibility to his fellow Indians to not only convey the right impression of Islam but also embody the principles of nationalism deemed correct by the majority. You have to be an exemplary, upright and righteous individual; people are going to look at you and judge other Muslims based on your conduct. I have to be on my guard all the time because I know people are looking, and they generally are going to associate any actions I do as a representative of my religion.

We're all ambassadors of whatever we are. You're an ambassador to your faith and society as you live your lives. It is not what you profess or preach that matters; it is finally your actions that define you and your thoughts. Your public perception is built over some time and is shaped by the uniformity of your speech and behaviour.

A dichotomous behaviour is bound to erode your credibility, and your loyalty to your faith can very well be misperceived as disloyalty to national values. The cardinal values that underpin your faith and your patriotism are normally shared by each other: ethical conduct and pluralist character.

It is worth quoting Dr. S. Radhakrishnan, the philosopher-President of India, 'What counts is not creed but conduct. By their fruits, ye shall know them and not by their beliefs. Religion is not a correct belief but righteous living. The Hindu view that every method of spiritual growth, and every path to the Truth is worthy of reverence has much to commend itself (*The Hindu View of Life*, 1962).'

There's always a certain level of bias initially when people meet you. I think that the main challenge is having those conversations and getting people to a level where they stop seeing you just as a Muslim, but as a fellow Indian and a person of faith. It is equally true that in recent times the highly volatile and hostile environment has made the situation very complicated. Proffering advice is easier said than done.

Being Muslim and being Indian are compatible and go hand-in-hand. You don't need to compromise your faith to prove your patriotism; real patriotism is demonstrated through the timeless values of Indian civilisation — fairness, justice, tolerance, and pluralism.

We are reminded of the writings of the great author Amin Maalouf on Identity. In re-reading them, I realised I had forgotten how relevant his thinking is for the times in which we live. Written in 1998, Maalouf says:

[In] the age of globalisation and of the ever-accelerating intermingling of elements in which we are all caught up, a new concept of identity is needed and needed urgently. We cannot be satisfied with forcing billions of bewildered human beings to choose between the excessive assertion of their identity and the loss of their identity altogether, between fundamentalism and disintegration. But that is the logical consequence of the prevailing attitude on the subject.

If our contemporaries are not encouraged to accept their multiple affiliations and allegiances, if they cannot reconcile their needs for identity with an open and unprejudiced tolerance of other cultures; if they feel as if they need to choose between the denial of self and the denial of the other - then we shall be bringing into being legions of the lost and hordes of bloodthirsty madmen.

For it is the way we look at other people that imprisons them within their own narrowest allegiances. And it is also the way we look at them that may set them free.

Many admired Maulana Azad's commitment to Hindu-Muslim unity. It all started when he was 16 or 17 and joined the guerrilla movement called Jugantar in Bengal. That commitment continued until the end of his life when he addressed terrified Muslims on the brink of mass exodus to the newly-created state of Pakistan. On December 15, 1947, from the steps of the Jama Masjid in Delhi, he said to the crowds, "Where are you going and why?"

When the Partition Resolution was on the table, three men of conscience refused to sign it: Gandhiji, Khan Abdul Ghaffar Khan and Maulana Azad. The Pathan spoke seven words to his comrades, words that were emblazoned on the heart of every Indian: "You are throwing us to the wolves." Azad spoke four words: "Over my dead body." Gandhi's anguish was palpable, but being the Mahatma, he bowed before his friends and the die was cast.

This was 24 years after Azad, as the youngest Congress President, spoke these immortal words at the session in Delhi on December 15, 1923: "If an angel were to descend from heaven and declare that India would get Swaraj in 24 hours, provided she relinquishes Hindu-Muslim unity, I will answer, 'Never'. If Swaraj is delayed, it will be a loss for India, but if Hindu-Muslim unity is lost, it will be a loss to humanity."

Hindu-Muslim ittehad (unity) is at stake as never before. The angel has descended and made his declaration, but he has been shown his place. Indians are being swept by a tsunami of hate.

Muslims are faced with a dilemma of dichotomous loyalties, and the best inspiration for them in these trying times is Maulana Azad, who was the President of the Indian National Congress during the negotiation of independence and was a key ally of Gandhi and Nehru. He wrote:

I am a Musalman and am proud of that fact. Islam's splendid traditions of 1,300 years are my inheritance. I am unwilling to lose even the smallest part of this inheritance. The teaching and history of Islam, its arts and letters, and civilisation, are my wealth and my fortune. I must protect them.

As a Musalman, I have a special interest in Islamic religion and culture, and I cannot tolerate any interference with them. But in addition to these sentiments, I have others also which the realities and conditions of my life have forced upon me. The spirit of Islam does not come in the way of these sentiments; it guides and helps me forward.

I am proud of being an Indian. I am part of the indivisible unity that is Indian nationality. I am indispensable to this noble edifice, and without me, this splendid structure of India is incomplete. I am an essential element that has gone to build India. I can never surrender this claim.

It was India's historic destiny that many human races and cultures and religions should flow to her, finding a home in her hospitable soil, and that many a caravan should find rest here. Even before the dawn of history, these caravans trekked into India, and wave after wave of newcomers followed. This vast and fertile land gave welcome to all and took them to her bosom. One of the last of these caravans, following the footsteps of its predecessors, was that of the followers of Islam.

They came here and settled here for good.

India has been a flag bearer of pluralism and has always held the candle of tolerance, mutual respect, and peaceful coexistence. Muslims have, time and again, responded to the challenges of the nation, and facts and history attest to their role in building this great nation. Alienating one-fifth of this population will not help the country and will be against the spirit of its centuries-old ethos.

Collaboration between Communities

We need to have a collective goal to harness the power of collaboration to build a more sustainable, resilient, tolerant, and united community. This goal and its success depend considerably on bridging cultures. Beyond geographical spreads, bridging cultures is to rise above personal and professional challenges to provide foundational support systems ultimately. Essentially, it starts and extends with creating shared value formations within and beyond organizations to generate greater societal benefits. We must campaign to bring about a shift in our perspectives on the issues that matter and create a better world. To create long-term change, we must spread ideas that have the power to evolve communities and societies.

As continuing poverty and inequality challenge our nations, we have to harness the very best of human nature — generosity, innovation, creativity — to make the biggest possible difference in people's lives. We need to commit to helping build a more peaceful, equitable, and sustainable world for generations to come.

We can collaborate to form a unique group and combine our efforts to solve some of the greatest and most intractable challenges of our time. Collaboration has the power to deliver extraordinary progress. It can fight poverty, empower women, develop communities, and provide emergency help to those who need it most. Just as importantly, it also has the power to bridge the divides that exist between different cultures around the world. We have to harness the very best of human nature – generosity, innovation, creativity – to make the biggest possible difference in people's lives across nations.

The Tinderbox of the Uniform Civil Code and Gender Equality in Islam

The discourse over the implementation of the Uniform Civil Code has often stirred up a whirlwind of uproar by political advocates and religious objectors. India follows a system of legal pluralism that allows different religious communities to be governed by their codes of personal law. This has been seen as a way of protecting distinct communal identities and safeguarding the right of citizens to practice their faith, as enshrined in the Constitution.

The Constitution grants equal protection under the law to all citizens. That said, Muslims are governed by a personal law, which came into force in 1937. However, the authors of the Constitution wanted a common set of family laws. Article 44 of the Directive Principles of State Policy in the Indian Constitution mandates that "the state shall endeavour to secure for all citizens a Uniform Civil Code throughout the territory of India."

The Uniform Civil Code (UCC) calls for the formulation of one law for India which would apply to all religious communities in matters such as marriage, divorce, inheritance, and adoption. Because of the intrepid opposition of Muslim members, the idea was dropped, but the issue was not sealed. It was left to the wisdom of the coming generations to explore the concept of a generic set of personal laws -- a Uniform Civil Code (UCC) applicable to all Indians.

The authors of the Constitution had realised that Muslims were stubborn about retaining their laws, and the time was not ripe for the fruition of a Common Civil Code. One of the active participants in the debate who played a crucial role in shaping the discourse was Kazi Syed Karimuddin, who represented CP and Berar province in the Constituent Assembly and was a leading criminal lawyer at Yavatmal.

Kazi Syed Karimuddin was born on 19 July 1899 in Yavatmal, Maharashtra. He obtained a law degree from Aligarh Muslim University and became a notable litigator. Karimuddin was elected to the Constituent Assembly from the Central Provinces through a Muslim League ticket. In the Assembly, he made interventions on essential issues related to privacy, emergency provisions, and proportional representation. Karimuddin was a Member of the Rajya Sabha (1954-1958).

On this issue, the Assembly was divided into two parts: on one side, there were people like KM Munshi and MaulanaHasratMohani. Muslim members of the Assembly believed that the protection of personal laws must be a priority. Consequently, a majority of 5:4 of the subcommittee on Fundamental Rights decided that UCC should not be adopted as a Fundamental Right.

Dr. Ambedkar said that we do not want to lay down certain principles because it would open the coming generations to have their pattern. It is only stated in Article 31 that there will be an improvement in economic, social, and other things. What is the use of generalisations, as expressed in Article 31? Therefore, it is no use treating these principles as Directive; such a course will not prove to be for the good of the people and the State. All these principles must be made mandatory so that a scheme embodying these principles can be brought into operation within ten years.

The Supreme Court struck a note of caution in the SarlaMudgal judgement. The court stated, "The desirability of a uniform civil code can be hardly doubted, but it can concretise only when the social climate is properly built by the elite of the society and the statesmen, instead of gaining personal mileage, rise above and awaken the masses to accept the change."

The Law Commission, acting on a reference made by the government in 2016, had, on August 31, 2018, floated a consultation paper on the Reform of Family Law. The consultation paper covered marriage and divorce, custody and guardianship, adoption and maintenance, and succession and inheritance.

In the 185-page consultation paper, the Commission has dealt with discriminatory laws "rather than providing a Uniform Civil Code which is neither necessary nor desirable at this stage."

The Commission stated in the consultation paper: "While the diversity of Indian culture can and should be celebrated, specific groups or weaker sections of society must not be disprivileged. The resolution of this conflict does not mean the abolition of difference. The Commission has, therefore, dealt with discriminatory laws rather than providing a UCC."

We must all understand that Islamic laws are far from being a rigid set of injunctions or rules set in stone. Islamic law or Shar'ia (meaning "way" or "path") is an immense amalgam of texts and interpretations that have evolved along parallel paths within five major and numerous minor schools of law.

Shari'a is a religious code for Muslims that covers all aspects of their life, including daily routines, and religious and familial obligations, marital affairs such as marriage and divorce, and financial dealings. Gender-just reforms are needed to help in correcting gender biases but they should be well-intentioned.

The reform backers believe that the state should undertake them, to use the words of the great parliamentarian Edmund Burke, with "the cold neutrality of an impartial judge." And by Burke's own words, "No man can mortgage his injustice as a pawn for his fidelity." The state cannot expect Muslims to jettison the core tenets of their faith. For Muslims, changes to Islamic law have to be made within the boundaries of the Quran's teachings if they are to be legitimate. Without the cooperation of the religious scholars, who bestow this legitimacy, the masses will not embrace change. The clerics are critical in the whole equation. The predominant hardliners among their ranks are locked in a virtual and civil war with reformers.

Islam may not always be the sole factor in the repression of women. Local, social, political, economic, and educational forces, as well as the prevalence of pre-Islamic customs, must also be taken into consideration.

A common civil code is being oversold as a silver bullet for gender justice, which it is not. In some societies, they are a pervasive influence. But, in many cases, the proper application of Islamic law remains a major obstacle to the evolution of the position of women.

Muslims are apprehensive of the state's obsession with trying to "create" a specific type of Islam, rather than allowing them space to simply live Islam – with all its beliefs, traditions, cultures, references, and various practices.

UCC can't guarantee the empowerment of women. They see the civil code as a seductively wrapped gender welfare intervention that can be a powerful salient, paving the way for further intrusion into their religious and cultural values. This slippery slope is not lost on Muslims who see it as slouching toward a pernicious future for their faith. The depressing social conditions of Muslim women are a phenomenon prevalent mostly among the underprivileged.

In economically improved strata of Muslims, the sort of oppressive practices that are being talked about are a rarity. Poverty is the root cause of obscurantism in Muslim families. Economic empowerment is one tide that can lift all the boats. It enables you to provide better education, better housing, and better healthcare. It is a virtual cycle that transforms your worldview. The biggest problems facing Muslim women today are economic. They are not likely to be solved with civil rights remedies, but they could be relieved with public and private action to encourage economic redevelopment. More than religious redemption, women need economic redemption.

What is urgently required is draining the swamps of Muslim poverty that are breeding unrest and frustration, leading to both physical and mental violence.

The opponents argue that those averse to customary law have several options. There are already several laws like the Indian Marriage Act, Indian Divorce Act, Indian Succession Act, and Indian Wards & Guardianship Act, which provide a secular alternative for those who want it. This law allows Indians to marry and be governed by secular civil laws, irrespective of the faith followed by either party. Therefore, there is no need to impose on everyone a secular civil code.

Muslim women leaders are convinced that Islam, at its core, is progressive for women and supports equal opportunities for men and women alike. They would not like to wager for a law that makes them jettison their Islamic beliefs.

Deeply religious, profoundly determined, and modern in every way, they are challenging not only the unjust restrictions placed on them by their societies. But they also oppose the tired stereotypes and empty generalisations placed on them by the West. They are arguing for women's rights within an Islamic discourse.

These women are combing through centuries of Islamic jurisprudence to cull out and highlight the more progressive aspects of their religion. Muslim women leaders are seeking accommodation between a modern role for women and the Islamic values that more than a billion people in the world follow. Some of the leading proponents are men—distinguished scholars who contend that Islam was radically egalitarian for its time and remains so in many of its texts.

Muslims are well integrated in Sri Lanka, where they have their law, which has been lauded by jurists. Singapore and Israel accept Muslim personal law.

AharonLayish wrote a paper in July 1973 on "The Shar'ia in Israel." Israel's Shar'ia court system is more efficient than the civil law alternative. It is also evolving in conjunction with the demands of an 'open, modern, and developed' society. Israel's religious courts feature as part of the judicial system, with applicants having the option of choosing whether to lodge cases in the religious or civil courts. Shar'ia courts in Israel are informed by the Hanafi legal school of Sunni jurisprudence, while laws in place since the days of the Ottoman Empire also remained in force.

There is a need to reassess. Reform is an unruly horse that can go berserk unless it is properly saddled. The modern trend is for the acceptance of diversity. It is equally important for the Muslim theocracy to understand their proper role, call it religious policing, cultural policing, guardian policing, family policing, and community policing.

www.ingramcontent.com/pod-product-compliance
Lightning Source LLC
LaVergne TN
LVHW041112150826
845673LV00007B/2023

* 9 7 9 8 8 9 2 7 7 8 7 6 3 *